FIRING THE
FLYING SCOTSMAN
AND OTHER GREAT
LOCOMOTIVES

FIRING THE FLYING SCOTSMAN
AND OTHER GREAT LOCOMOTIVES

Life on the Footplate in the Last Years of Steam

KEN ISSITT
ILLUSTRATED BY CHRIS BATES

The
History
Press

For Alice Starmore
1886 – 1985

First published 2012

The History Press
The Mill, Brimscombe Port
Stroud, Gloucestershire, GL5 2QG
www.thehistorypress.co.uk

British Library Cataloguing in Publication Data.
A catalogue record for this book is available from the British Library.

ISBN 978 0 7524 8043 5

Typesetting and origination by The History Press
Printed in Great Britain

CONTENTS

ACKNOWLEDGEMENTS

When I sat down to write my thank yous I thought it would be an easy job. It turned out to be a thought-provoking exercise. I do not intend to list my thanks but rather to offer my thoughts.

When I started to write this book, illustrating had not occurred to me. It was only when I was telling Chris, who plays sax alongside me in a swing band, what I was doing and he said that he was an artist that it suddenly dawned on me that I could ask him to illustrate the book. And that is what he has done.

Chris did not know about footplate life with all that it entailed. I told him about some of the things that happened to me during my time on the footplate and since then he has made it his business to become familiar with steam locomotives, visiting the Midland Mainline Steam Trust, asking questions and taking photographs so that he could get the feel as much as possible of bygone railway days. Chris has drawn his sketches in the genre of the fifties, the time in which my stories are set. My thanks go to Chris.

Between us – at times in the vernacular and at times in the traditions of storytellers – we have tried to bring the stories to life.

So many people are enthused by the steam locomotive. The romance of trains steaming through the countryside seems to be in our collective memory. There is, too, a resurgence of interest. Booksellers have magazines on their shelves; even garden centres have books about steam trains. This can be seen in the request for stories about the *Flying Scotsman*, the writing about which inspired me to write about other things that happened to me in the 1950s. So in saying thank you I realise that my contribution to this scene

If we found ourselves stationary we were waiting to go somewhere

was to write about my time on the railway in which I was actively involved. My thanks are to all the people who from my recollections and subsequent connections have helped to rekindle my interest in steam locomotives. The response that Chris and I have had from the talks we have given has always been warm. Trips on the private railways and the volunteers who give their time, the popularity of York Railway Museum, and the building of the new steam locomotive *Tornado* all play a part in contributing to the scene into which my stories are set.

I had received a pamphlet from Eric Maxwell Bryce, a railway employee and lifelong railway enthusiast. Included in the pamphlet was a request for stories about the *Flying Scotsman* from York Museum. As I had earned my living on the footplate of that engine from time to time I was prompted to reply, so I am grateful to Max.

My thanks also go to Professor Rob Coles of the University of Leicester for his helpful and constructive comments.

My overwhelming gratitude goes to my sons Stephen, John and Michael. As a young boy Stephen knew more about the comings and goings of railway engines than I ever did, as he was an avid trainspotter.

My thanks also go to an ex-colleague, Ron Hefford; to Chris's Sue, who posed for many of the action drawings for Chris; to the late Gerald Boden, who kindly allowed Chris to climb over his LNER B1 steam engine *Mayflower* to take photographs; and thanks go to Jean Bryce, who patiently dotted the i's and crossed the t's. Specially, I would like to thank Margaret, my wife, whose comments such as 'You can't write that; it doesn't make sense!' made me realise that my feeble attempts to join the army of writers needed a bit more than just checking out in the dictionary to see whether a word had been spelt correctly. Margaret has been my driving force in all this. She has helped me understand that what I have done has been worthwhile. I couldn't have done it without her.

So my thank you is to all the people who have contributed in any way – thank you!

LIST OF ILLUSTRATIONS

Backstage

Another Right Mess

Attempted Murder?

Eggs and Bluelegs

End Note

I Remember as if it was Yesterday

1

WHAT DO YOU WANT TO BE WHEN YOU GROW UP?

'**You tell a** good tale, don't you?' someone said to me recently. This brought me up with a start. I was telling a lady a story about my railway years that was perfectly true, with all sincerity. She clearly did not believe me. It made me recall a previous incident in which I had related the story Put the Kettle On and Shout up the Stairs! (chapter 7) to some young people I had met in a pub one evening. I was disconcerted to realise that they clearly did not believe me either.

All the tales in this book are true. The only documentary evidence I have in my possession is a witness report relevant to the story that I have entitled Jigsaws (chapter 5). The reader will appreciate that there will be evidence elsewhere, perhaps in the annals of railway history. But I have concentrated on the stories themselves; about incidents that happened to me. I am sure, however, that many railwaymen could relate dramatic events that happened to them: life on the footplate was full of drama.

The locomotive crew took risks with their own safety every day; the danger was part of the job, perhaps even the appeal of it. The men were expected to use common sense every moment of the day. Each story contains elements of these risks. It does not seem possible to make a direct comparison between life on the footplate in the 1950s and that experienced by train crews today. The use of different sources of power – oil and electricity – and the development of digital technology have completely transformed the footplate. The present-day driver does not have a fireman who performs the duties explained in this book. He/she has a different set of responsibilities as the train is driven along the same tracks that were laid

'What do you want to be when you grow up?'

many years ago. There is legislation that both supports and controls the daily duties of the crew.

I was fortunate to work as a fireman on some notable steam locomotives in the final years of steam. As the steam era slid into history the work of the fireman as it was ceased. In 1965 steam was replaced by diesel and electricity as forms of traction by British Rail. The driver/fireman relationship on a steam locomotive, a relationship that had existed for years, was no longer there.

This is not a book about observing the workings of the footplate crew; it is a book about a fireman doing his job. A mere observer would see the discomforts of the train crew – the heat, the dust, the knocks – but he would also know that he, as an observer, did not actually experience them. I did.

The stories also offer an historical perspective on the job of being a fireman. In recording them I hope to go some way towards giving an account of the life and work of a footplate crew in the final years of steam. Perhaps, too, I am able to bring that to life through my stories.

I worked on the footplate from 1947 to 1960 and of course I am only writing about what happened to me. Some railwaymen gave their entire working life to service on the footplate and my contribution was small in comparison. I am sure that many footplate incidents have gone unrecorded. I hope that in relating these stories I will help fill what I consider to be a gap in the history of footplate work.

I have tried to illustrate the life we led from day to day, from the fairly routine to the downright hazardous. It was always one of movement; if we found ourselves stationary we were waiting to go somewhere. It was a moving job. You had to make the engine shift and fulfil its task. You needed to know your engine so that when it was asked to perform you made sure that everything had been done for maximum efficiency. Engines had their own personality and their own life, sometimes happy and sometimes mardy.

We all had our favourite engines. *Galtee More* (an A3 Pacific) was my favourite. She was easy to get to steam and full working pressure and I could even take liberties with her. We could start away with less than a good body of lit coal in the firebox. *Galtee More* was a free-steaming engine and responded very quickly. But you dare not take liberties with some engines where you needed a really good start with everything on your side. The boiler needed to be fairly full and have a good head of steam. All engines, however, had to be prepared ready for the journey with the fire bright, so that when the regulator was opened by the driver a full head of steam was in the steam chest, and the water in the boiler was at the right level. The fireman and the guard would then watch the train safely out of the station precincts. They then returned to their prime duties – the fireman to that of firing the engine correctly and maintaining the water level in the boiler and the guard to the train itself and the welfare of the passengers.

My sixteen shifts (a.m./p.m.) – one week a.m. and one week p.m. for sixteen weeks – meant it was extremely difficult to socialise. It was hard to plan anything either for my family or myself. I could not, for instance, take a course at night school, join a football team or attend anything that involved regular commitment. Every shift started at a different time: 12.01a.m. was regarded as a day shift, and 10p.m. a night shift. These timings were related to the times of the trains throughout the night and day.

I considered that the best shift in the 'fast train link', of which I was a member, was: book on duty at 7.40a.m., work the Master Cutler to London, leaving at 9.19a.m. and arriving at 11.24a.m.; then bring the 12.15p.m. dinnertime fast back to Leicester from Marylebone, arriving in Leicester at 2.40p.m. When I had done that I could be watching *Bill and Ben the Flowerpot Men* on the television with my family at home in the late afternoon.

I always had a canvas bag which I put on my back as I rode to work on my bike. Inside I had sandwiches, sometimes an apple, a mashing of tea, milk in a Camp coffee bottle and a screw of sugar. This all fitted, with the enamel tea can, neatly into the bag.

The Great Central and the Great Northern Railway engine sheds at Leicester were situated in two locations. One, serving the Great Central line, was at the southern end of the city and was close to the canal that flows through Leicester, connecting with the River Soar. The other served the Great Northern line and was approximately 2 miles away. They were constructed of brick and completed in the latter part of the nineteenth century. The Great Central shed, the major and the larger of the two, had four bays housing about thirty engines, depending on their size. Four bays, with a gap between each, meant that the shed area would be about the size of a football pitch. The smaller shed had only two bays. When I approached the sheds on my way to work I was always struck by the shape of the roof, as the shed architecture included a series of scalene triangles across the whole length of the shed. To the right of the engine bays there was a shed master's office. Alongside that was a walkway that gave access to the enginemen's lobby and the running foreman's office, the loco crews' mess room, the stores department, the blacksmith's shop and the boiler cleaning section, the machine shop with several lathes and drilling machines, the fitters' shop, and finally the fitters' mess room. General maintenance was done 'in house'. These sections ran the whole length of the engine shed.

You had to make the engine shift and fulfil its task

'Booking on' happened in the stores department. I would tell the storesman, whose name was Mac, that I was there. After booking me on duty Mac issued me with the appropriate kit for the engine allocated to us. That meant a shovel, a coal hammer, a bucket, a gauge lamp, detonators, a hand brush and some hand cloths. It was here that I was told which engine we were to work that day and where that engine was standing. This would usually be on the shed front of one of four bays, ready for our departure to the station. After booking on, my driver would read the essential notices in the enginemen's lobby about speed restrictions, single line working, fitters' reports, line repairs and anything pertaining to the track for our journey that day. Then he would sign the Road Book, which meant that he took responsibility for the safety of the locomotive and the train that he was about to drive to and from its destination.

I was now 'booked on'. Eventually it would be my turn as a new driver to examine the notices. When a fireman was approaching the time for him to pass his exams to be a driver he would be notified by the company. As well as studying his rule book and making himself conversant with all the aspects of engine working and the rules and regulations required of him, he would also need to know how to drive the engine correctly in the different situations he might encounter. For instance, driving a shunting engine means working closely with a 'shunter' when assembling a goods train. He would have to know that driving a loose-coupled train required a completely different technique to driving a passenger train with a continuous brake, what these differences were and how to deal with them including the knowledge of what to do in case of a breakdown or signal failure. No driver was obliged to hand over the controls to a budding driver but most drivers would give their fireman a chance at the controls if only for a short distance. In reality, of course, over the years a fireman would get the opportunity to switch positions with the different drivers with whom he was rostered. Some became great friends. I was most fortunate with my last driver. He let me drive all the local passenger trains and he drove all the fast passenger trains. I was very grateful to him for allowing me to gain this valuable experience. He was confident I wouldn't let him down and I made sure I didn't.

2

ON A NORMAL SHIFT – LEICESTER TO LONDON AND RETURN

The route to London from Leicester is known as the 'up line' and the return route is known as the 'down line'. I have chosen to describe a crew's experience of a typical shift on an A3 Pacific from Leicester to London in the 1950s, 'on the up' and back 'on the down', to illustrate a day's work. The driver books on duty in the stores department and so does the fireman. The storesman tells them which engine they are to work that day and where the engine is berthed. The driver goes to the engineman's lobby and signs the Road Book. He is signing that he is competent to take charge and is perfectly familiar with that route, the signals, junctions and stations during the day or night. The driver familiarises himself with the appendices and notices that are relevant to the route that he knows he will be working. The fireman also has access to these notices. They would include speed restrictions, diversions, track repairs and fitters' reports about the engine the crew is about to work. The fireman goes to the stores and draws the shovel, coal hammer, bucket, gauge lamp, detonators, hand brush and hand cloths. He then takes the kit to the engine.

The driver himself goes to the stores and he draws two types of oil. One is to lubricate the big end crankshafts, the side rods, the valve gear and the oil keeps. An oil keep in this instance is a container for oil with pipes attached through which the oil is drip-fed to the slow-moving parts of the ancillary equipment around the framing above the driving wheels. The other type of oil is heavy engine oil (black oil) for the mechanical lubricators that feed the valves and pistons that get extremely hot as the engine is being worked. It is the driver's prime job to oil the engine.

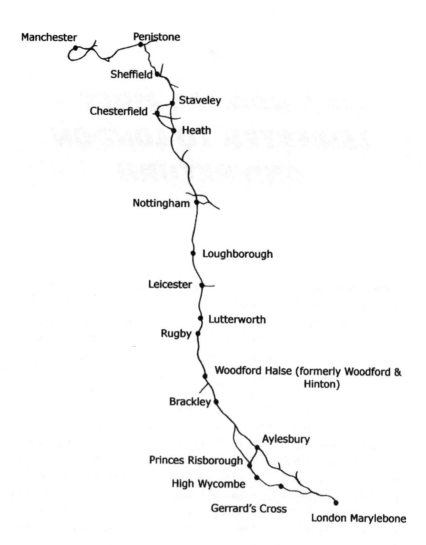

Map of Great Central Line from Manchester to London

The driver then gradually works around the engine oiling the various moving parts. The fireman assists the driver with these oiling duties by filling the lubricators on the framing above the driving wheels. Whilst he is on the framing he makes sure that the sandboxes are full and the smokebox is empty of ash and secure ready for the journey. This is known as 'preparing for the journey'. On an A3 Pacific the fireman usually has an extra job. The driver will position the engine so that the fireman will be able to reach the middle big end journal. This is underneath the engine and can only be reached from the inspection pit that is about 3ft deep. The fireman has to stoop as he moves along the inspection pit. After he has reached the middle crankshaft with the oilcan in his hand he can stand almost upright and unscrew the tapered cork from the top of the big end journal. He can fill up the journal, which is part of the crankshaft, with oil and then replace the cork. Occasionally the motion of the big end when the engine is racing along causes a cork to fly out. A driver will have one or two spare corks in his pocket in case this happens. All moving parts of an engine are coated with oil so it is difficult for the fireman to keep it off his overalls when he is doing this job. I was always aware that if another engine came up behind us and touched our buffers as I was squashed underneath the motions, I would be crushed.

An hour is allowed for this work. Sometimes, however, the engine is already prepared for the train crew by the shed staff. It is all oiled up, coaled up, the footplate cleaned and the tender filled with coal and water. Only a short time, twenty minutes, is allowed for the driver to look at the notices and for the fireman to make sure that everything he needs is on the footplate.

The driver checks that both the vacuum brake and the steam brake are working properly; the fireman checks that the appropriate tools for cleaning the fire are on the tender – that is, the long fire shovel (for removing clinker and hot ash from the firebox), the straight dart (for breaking up the clinker) and the bent dart (for spreading the fire around the firebox). It is also his job to climb on to the tender and fill up the tank with water from the water column alongside the engine. The engine will be set against the columns ready for this. Whilst on the tender he will make sure that the coal is properly stacked and there is no likelihood of pieces of coal falling from the tender on to the track. The fireman, satisfied that all his equipment is there, makes sure that the two detachable headlamps, which are always fitted to the engine, have trimmed wicks and keeps that are full of paraffin. The gauge lamp also has to be trimmed. This is to illuminate the water level in the sight glass on the footplate. The headlamps are positioned in the following way: one is placed on the framing above the buffers on the front of the engine and one is similarly placed on the back of the tender. The latter has to be a red light; the one on the front is white, so that the front and the back of the engine are illuminated at night. When the train is attached to the engine the rear light will be removed and placed on the front of the engine. This headlamp arrangement, of a white light on each front buffer, means that this is a fast train. The shade in the lamp will be altered to give a white light.

The last thing the crew does before leaving the loco sheds for the station is to clean up the footplate. This will be their place of work for the next few hours. The cockpit of a plane and the bridge on a ship are two examples of places where people spend their days in the service of others. The footplate is no exception. The crew do not know what is before them as they climb on board. When the crew first gets on to the engine, it is grimy and smoky. That is because when steam is being raised in the engine by the 'steam riser', who will have been on the footplate first to do this job, fumes and smoke fill the footplate until the time when sufficient steam is raised to operate the blower jet. This is usually about 50 psi on the steam pressure gauge. When the crew takes over, the blower jet is operational. It produces an induced draught on the contents of the firebox and therefore keeps the flames and smoke in the firebox itself. The driver and the fireman clean their respective sides of the footplate, including the front and side windows to give clear visibility in places where coal dust collects – particularly on the driver's side where there are nooks and crannies. Between them they make the footplate habitable by spraying hot water over it from the degger pipe to lay down all the dust, not forgetting the seats. This pipe is fitted on the low pressure side of the boiler and allows hot water to pass through it. It is controlled by a little hand valve on the fireman's side of the engine.

There are two lockers on a footplate and they are situated on the tender. One is for the oilcans and detonators and the other for food and clothing.

A regular express train driver will almost certainly be in his late fifties. He will have an experienced fireman with him who will need no prompting. This man will know when to start firing the engine, when to stop firing, when to check for signals – in fact, he will be conversant with all the many duties he is expected to do. The driver can then settle down to driving the engine correctly, taking note of all his arrival times for each station along the route. He will also attend to the efficient running of the engine, aiming to get the passengers to their destination on time.

The fireman will make up the fire in the firebox. He fills the back corners and the area under the fire hole door first, using a good ton of coal that will then gradually burn through and be all ready for when he needs to spread

Oiling and checking the engine in the shed

Filling the tender with water

the hot coals all over the firebox itself with the bent dart. This is when full steam pressure is required for the engine to pull the coaches and take the weight of the train. The ideal requirements for the train to pull away is to have 225 psi of boiler pressure and a boiler that is nearly full. If the boiler is too full, water could get into the valves and pistons; 225 psi gives the engine maximum power.

The engine has to go tender first when travelling from the loco sheds to the station so that it is pointing in the correct direction. In this case it would be south – to London. This is termed 'light engine'. The short journey to the station takes the engine into a side bay. The engine stops there until the train arrives. The fireman gradually brings the engine round to full steam, just as the train arrives. He will prevent the engine from blowing off steam at the safety valve by putting an injector on to top up the boiler to the right level as the engine backs on to the train. After the engine on the incoming train has been disconnected from the carriages it is taken forward to the loco sheds. The driver on the London express will wait for the signal to rise so that he can leave the bay and duly back on to the train that is waiting for him. The signalman beckons to the driver when he has altered the points, to allow the engine to be backed on to the train. It's all a question of fine timing.

The driver backs the engine up and the shunter will usually couple up the engine to the train. If he is not available then the fireman does this. The shunter couples the engine up to the train with a screw coupling. The vacuum brake pipe will then be coupled up. This pipe runs from the engine through the whole of the train and controls the brake on every wheel. This works by the creation of a vacuum that is destroyed when the driver applies the brake, allowing air to rush into the brake pipe. As soon as that happens the brakes on every wheel go on. The steam heater pipe, on the other hand, is operated by a hand wheel on the faceplate on the fireman's side of the engine. Steam heat is passed to each carriage. The fireman removes the tail lamp from the tender, changing its colour to white, and takes it forward, placing it on the bracket mounted on the framing above the opposite buffer at the front of the engine.

During the day the fireman will watch for the guard's green flag and listen for his blow on the whistle. At night the fireman watches for a green light and also for the sound of the whistle. It is these that alert the fireman to give a pop on the engine whistle to acknowledge the guard's signals, with a 'Right away mate' to the driver. The fireman then watches the train safely out of the station precincts.

Leicester is in a dip in the landscape. The line to London from Leicester starts with a rise for several miles, levelling out somewhere past Lutterworth. Maximum power is required from an engine hauling an eleven-coach train to climb the gradients and no let-up in the engine's performance will occur until the train has passed Lutterworth when the track levels out. As the demand for steam from the boiler lessens, the driver can ease the regulator. A fireman will be firing constantly. The driver will be watching the steam pressure gauge and the water level in the boiler with three things in mind: first, to be on time at the next station (Rugby); second, to know how hard to push the engine to achieve this; and third, not to leave the engine with the steam pressure low and too little water in the boiler. Each of these aspects is necessary because if one of them were not attended to properly, the fireman would struggle to maintain both steam and water. This applies particularly on this route because it is a considerable distance from Rugby to the next stop, Aylesbury. Maximum effort on the part of the fireman is required. His technique to efficiently fire the engine and maintain the steam pressure is described as 'little and often'. A fireman will wait for the smoke from the engine chimney to start to change colour from white to dark grey; when the colour of the smoke coming from the chimney is evenly spread he will stop firing for a minute or two until the smoke clears. Too much heavy smoke tells the fireman he is not allowing the fuel to be burned at the correct rate. Then he repeats the exercise until the top of the gradient is reached. The fireman knows that the driver will further shorten the valve travel: the driver's skill is in his knowledge of how to economise the use of steam by what is called 'shortening the valve travel'. This conserves the passage of steam from the steam chest into the valves and pistons.

Watches were not issued and there were no speedometers. In order to keep to time it was in the interest of the driver to have a watch. The clocks in signal boxes and stations were illuminated at night and a driver without a watch would take his timing from them as he passed. On this run we would be going in daylight and returning in darkness. To have a watch made life easier. Further, when it was dark and also foggy the driver may not be able to see the clocks in the signal boxes and on stations.

The first stop is Rugby. There is a long run down into Rugby station, giving the fireman the opportunity to fill the boiler and get full steam ready for the next part of the journey. This is where the Central main line crosses the Midland line – both lines used for fast trains to London. This train, of course, is going to Marylebone; the Midland trains go to Euston.

Checking the connection
between engine and carriage

The line from Rugby to Aylesbury, having passed through several stations on the way, gradually climbs. It goes through Catesby Tunnel and approaches the water troughs where the tank is topped up.

There are two ways in which a locomotive takes on water. One is from a water column usually situated at the end of station platforms, and the other is via water troughs. On this journey to London the fireman would get water from the troughs at Charwelton in Northamptonshire. It would be his job to lower the water scoop as he approached the troughs. The handle for the scoop would be mounted on the tender. A further description of taking on water is described in Fog in the Fifties (chapter 10).

Aylesbury is our next stop. This is the last stop before London and the train is getting full. Again there is an uphill line for some miles and the line runs parallel with the Metropolitan line from Watford South Junction, only leaving this when entering the tunnels prior to getting to Marylebone station precincts. The driver is faced with a battery of coloured signals, many of which do not apply to him. He has to concentrate on recognising the signals he needs from the red, green, yellow and double yellow signals he can see. The driver controls the train into the station, bearing in mind that there is a set of hydraulic buffers mounted at the end of the platform. These are ready to absorb any shock if the driver approaches too fast and he is not able to stop. This is necessary because this is not a through station; this is the end of the line.

It is important to gradually 'run the fire down' as the train reaches its destination so that there is a minimum of steam and smoke in the station itself. It would be bad practice to have the engine blowing off steam while standing in the station and also a waste of fuel and water. As London Marylebone is a dead end station the crew has to wait until the station pilot comes to pull the train from the platform. This enables the crew to reverse out and go onto the turntable and ash pit. After cleaning the fire and filling the tank from the water column the fireman shovels coal forward on top of the tender ready for the return journey.

On arrival the driver immediately examines the engine as he did when he first came on duty. He oils side rods and crankshafts, topping up the keeps where he needs to. (It is rare that the engine has to be replaced on a journey such as this. A replacement engine would only be necessary if the driver considered that there was a serious overheating of one of the moving parts, such as the big ends or the valve gear.) He can then back up on to the train for its journey home.

It will be twilight by now. There is an opportunity before the start of the return journey to mash the tea and eat sandwiches. By the late 1950s there was variation in the fillings for sandwiches. The days of rationing and short supply had gone and using ham or beef could replace the cheese and pickle of earlier days.

The crew listens for the guard's whistle and his green light. A pop on the whistle acknowledges his signals and they draw the engine slowly out of the station, the fireman watching the train away from the platform.

Driving and firing an engine at night is different from daytime work. At night light is provided on the footplate by the glare of the firebox and the small light focused on the gauge lamp that indicates the level of the water in the boiler. The engine headlamps have to be lit, as does the gauge lamp on the footplate by the fireman. In the day the headlights mounted just above the buffers are unlit, but at night it is the fireman's job to light them. He would use either a match or a spill. The crew is not able to see the track ahead as clearly as they can during the daytime; figures are not clear, neither are animals. There is no powerful beam to illuminate the track in front of the engine, as a car would have with its headlights. Signals, however, are very visible. Whether they are powered by electricity or by oil they are all lit up.

The sensation of speed that the crew experiences alters when the train is travelling at night, although it is moving at the same speed as during the day. It is easy to think that the train is travelling much faster at night-time. During the day the crew can see the track ahead, but this is not so at night. Neither can the surrounding countryside be seen. It is like being in a capsule. An express train travelling across the land in the dark is often described as a fiery dragon, with smoke and fire belching into the darkness, and the image is etched in the memory. To the crew, to be part of that image adds an excitement to the journey.

The hills that we climbed on the journey up have become the gradients that we now go down. From the station at Marylebone the train enters tunnels that go uphill; that means the fireman is busy. The train emerges from the tunnels and is alongside the Metropolitan line. At night, of course, there are many signal and station lights, some applicable to the Metropolitan line and some applicable to us.

We run through Harrow, Rickmansworth and Watford South Junction where we part company with the Metropolitan line and continue towards Wendover and Aylesbury. Aylesbury is our first stop.

We stop at Aylesbury where passengers alight or board and proceed to Rugby, the next stop. Before this we have to take on water at Charwelton troughs. We shut off steam as we go through Catesby Tunnel, taking care to put the blower full on and to kick shut the trap on the fire door just before we enter the tunnel to prevent a blowback. Flames and smoke would fill the cab if the fire door was left open and a backpressure would be created between the top of the tunnel and the engine chimney.

There is a brief stop at Rugby so that passengers can leave the train and others can get on, and then we climb the final hill out of Rugby towards Leicester. There is a long run down from Ashby Magna, just past Lutterworth, to Leicester passenger station – an opportunity to run the fire down as the need for steam decreases.

As we reach the end of our journey the shunter will uncouple the engine from the train and we will make our way tender first from the station to the loco sheds, anchoring the engine down in the coal siding. The engine is now all ready to be coaled up in preparation for its next journey. We climb down from the footplate taking our kit with us to the stores and ask the storesman to sign us off. The driver goes to the engineman's lobby and makes a report about the engine, explaining any defects and mishaps, or anything that has occurred throughout the journey that needs putting in writing. Then we either stay for a while in the mess room to talk to fellow enginemen or we are homeward bound.

3

THE FLYING SCOTSMAN

Below is a copy of a letter I wrote to the National Railway Museum in York in December 2005 in answer to a request for stories about the *Flying Scotsman*. It contains an incident I had with this famous engine and forms the first story in this book.

To: National Railway Museum, York.

I read with interest your request for stories about the *Flying Scotsman*. As you say, every experience is unique and I appreciate the opportunity to tell you about one of the many things that happened whilst I was on the footplate. I was a fast train fireman when the engine was shedded at Leicester Central in the late fifties. Its number was changed to 60103, and another five Pacific locos also changed their numbers.

They came to Leicester Central to work fast trains – the Master Cutler, South Yorkshireman and other trains, such as the newspaper train from Marylebone to Nottingham, and those to Sheffield and Manchester. So I earned my living for several years on the *Flying Scotsman*, *Blink Bonny*, *Galtee More*, *Flying Fox*, *Solario* and another whose name escapes me.

The *Flying Scotsman* was never a free-steaming engine, so you knew when you booked on duty that you were going to have a hard day's firing. But that's how it was. Some days were harder than others. *Galtee More* (my favourite engine) was a free-steaming engine. You just had to show her the shovel and she steamed!

You asked for stories about the *Flying Scotsman*. Well here's a true drama that occurred in about 1958. My driver, Cyril, and I booked on duty to work

'Thank you for my safe journey'

the South Yorkshireman to London. I can't remember the exact date but it was summertime and very hot. There was a Maintenance Report on the engine saying that the injectors were faulty but had been put right ready for our journey.

Before we left the shed we went round to the coal stage to top up with more coal. That saved us getting coal down at London. We usually carried 8 tons of coal. We then travelled to the station to await the arrival of the South Yorkshireman. Sheffield men brought the train to Leicester, uncoupled their engine and moved onto the turntable. We backed on to the train, coupled up, and within minutes we had left the station and were on our way to London.

All went fairly well until we took water on from the troughs at Charwelton in Northamptonshire. We hit the troughs at speed and refilled the tank. Soon afterwards the right-hand injector began to leak water. I fiddled with it several times but kept having to supplement the boiler water with the left-hand injector. When the engine is working hard we had one injector on all the time and as we were pulling eleven coaches that day we were having to top up using the left-hand injector periodically. After we had passed Aylesbury the right-hand injector stopped working completely and the left-hand one began to play up. We had passed through Wendover, still maintaining time, when the left-hand injector also refused to work.

We had just climbed a fairly large gradient, so I had been busy firing. The engine was full of steam and the sight glass showed three quarters full and coming down. This was serious. Imagine your kettle on the stove with no water in it! We decided that the fire in the firebox had to come out p.d.q! Bear in mind that there is 41 square feet of grate area in the firebox and at least 2 tons of burning red-hot coal in there. I began to wind the grate down while Cyril struggled with the injector. He set the engine coasting with the regulator barely open. We happened to be going slightly downhill but we were blowing off steam at the safety valve, so losing boiler water. I finally wound down the grate and I took the long fire shovel from the tender. I began to push the fire from the firebox into the ash pan. We must have created quite a sight, as the red-hot fire pouring from the ash pan set the banks on either side of the track on fire with coal and cinders flying everywhere. As I opened the big fire door, the blast of heat actually took my breath away. It was a very hot day, and in the normal way you sweated a great deal. In this case, with the fire door wide open, believe me it was very warm. The long fire shovel was nearly white hot and beginning to bend as I pushed the fire through the grate. By this time the water level had disappeared in the glass.

We looked anxiously into the firebox to see if the lead plugs in its roof had melted and also for the telltale hiss of steam telling us how near we were to disaster. We were undoubtedly seconds away from an empty boiler and a near certain explosion. The engine was still blowing off steam when Cyril shouted, 'I've got it working!' 'Thank God,' I thought. We were still coasting at about 40mph, and still observing signals. It seemed like an age before the water appeared in the sight glass. We filled the boiler right up and I wound the grate back up again. I had probably shifted about half of the contents of the firebox so I was busy making the fire up again. I had read tales of engines blowing up in the early days of steam but as I was working like crazy I had no time to dwell on the prospects. Waiting for the water to appear brought these tales into my head. 'That was pretty close,' I thought. Fortunately there were no more big hills to climb so we nursed the *Flying Scotsman* for the last thirty miles or so to Marylebone, and were just five minutes late!

'Thank you for my safe journey,' said a lady passenger. Little did she know what had happened – or even what could have happened!

We dare not take the engine back to Leicester in the state she was in so we had to take the station pilot engine, a B1 mixed traffic engine, number 61028. It must have been the worst engine on British Railways. We had a hair-raising trip back – but that's another story.

The epilogue to this tale is that there was nothing wrong with the injectors. The engine was uncoupled from the tender for inspection and algae and rust were found to be blocking the strainers in the tender. Tenders of railway engines were rarely cleaned out and this one was obviously in need of maintenance. When the fitters drained the tender they also found three buckets of live fish – roach, bream, rudd – all swimming around happily and living off the algae in the tender. The water comes from the rivers, is pumped up to a large header tank, goes from there to the water columns and then to the tender. The bore of the pipes from the river is about 9in in diameter so little fish are easily sucked into the water system. Once in the tenders they just grow and multiply – a bit like a fishpond. If you think about it, a tender can never be empty when an engine is in steam, and if it were, there would be no water for the boiler. As long as there are a few inches or so of water in the tender the fish are happy.

When we did actually get home Cyril said he thought we had earned a pint. 'Don't you think so, mate?' he said.

This was just another day in the life of a footplate man, when every day held something different – different engine, different weather, different route, different driver, night work, day work, early morning shifts, afternoon shifts,

They also found three buckets of live fish

good trips, bad trips. I never tired of going to work and saw every engine as a challenge. I left the railway in 1960 when all the fast trains were removed from the Central line, a line that finally closed in 1965.

I was encouraged by the interest I received from York. This is what Joe Savage, the Exhibition Developer, replied:

Cyril said he thought we had earned a pint

'Your story is a fantastic resource, both for the *Flying Scotsman* files (with the brilliant twist of 4472 having the fish in the tender) and our forthcoming exhibition projects interpreting the lives of railway workers. The report of the day's events is both exciting and well written. Thank you for supporting our research. Stories like yours are rarely published.'

It spurred me on when I found it difficult to put my book together. In attempting to join the ranks of writers I now readily acknowledge their skills, so many of which I had taken for granted. I have, however, had the most enjoyable time presenting to the reader what was a special time for me. The letter to York began it all.

4

THE NIGHT THE FIRE WENT OUT

This tale is about how one thing affects another. Whenever I tell it I find the audience entirely sympathetic to my situation and wondering how I dealt with it.

It was one Sunday evening in early summer in the mid-1950s when a passenger train arrived at Leicester Central station from Sheffield on its way to London. My driver and I were scheduled to take this train the rest of the way. There was a fairly large crowd of people waiting on the platform, some of them with the camping gear and cycles that I knew would go into the guard's van. Perhaps they would be getting off at Rugby or Aylesbury, or even going all the way to London. Camping, cycling and youth hostelling were very popular then.

This was the last passenger train that night to London and our engine – a B1 mixed traffic engine – was waiting for us on the loco shed front, all coaled up to travel the half a mile or so to the station to await the arrival of our train. After booking on duty and going through the usual preliminaries of checking that we had the necessary tools – shovel, coal hammer, gauge lamp, hand brush, bucket, detonators, cloth wipes – we made our way to the station ready for the changeover. Our engine had been used on a goods train the day before in Colwick in Nottinghamshire, a goods depot. Colwick is a distance of 30 or so miles from Leicester.

At that time coal was not at all plentiful and goods depots had to put up with poor coal and also with briquettes. The briquettes were made from coal dust and cement. Not so at Leicester, as this was a fast train depot and good-quality coal such as Yorkshire Main was used. We rarely got inferior coal or briquettes. This particular day our engine had been coaled up from the hopper in Colwick.

When she arrived she was taken to our coal stage and topped up with Yorkshire Main for us to work the train to London. We left the loco sheds for the station ready to take the train forward. It duly arrived and after the Sheffield men had uncoupled their engine and made their way onto the turntable in the station precincts, we backed up on to the train and set off on our journey stopping at Rugby, Aylesbury and London.

After we left Rugby I realised I had used up all the Yorkshire Main. Briquettes and coal dust appeared to be all that remained on the tender. The engine continued to steam well, however, but only whilst we were working it hard and keeping a good blast on the fire. We were hauling eleven coaches at the time. The minute we arrived in London and stopped I looked into the firebox. The fire was a dull grey colour. It looked dead on the top.

We were not unduly concerned as we had a good three hours before we returned to Leicester. Eventually, the carriages were pulled away from us and we were able to run onto the turntable and then to the ash pit to clean the fire. Rocker fire bars were fitted to B1 mixed traffic engines, so with a special bar that was kept on the footplate you rocked the fire bars to break up the clinker in the firebox; then with the aid of the long fire shovel you pushed the ash into the ash pan and cleaned out the fire. I rocked the grates but I couldn't keep the fire alight with just coal dust and a few briquettes. There seemed to be no substance in the fuel. Then the fire went completely out. We managed to creep round to the hopper in the station precincts to get coal.

I knew that because we had had a good head of steam there was sufficient steam in the boiler to enable us to move a short distance. An engine will hold residual steam for a while if the engine is not being used, but I knew that as soon as we started to move the engine we would be losing the steam that was in the boiler. To our consternation we discovered that the hopper was locked up. Normally engines were not coaled from there until later on in the day and this was about twelve o'clock on a Sunday night. We had to alert the station staff that we needed coal urgently. Had we had sufficiently good coal I could have generated some steam and we could have taken the engine back and refuelled at Neasden loco, about 4 miles away. But the situation was that the fire was out, we had barely 150 psi of steam in the boiler and there was no chance of getting to Neasden. We would not have even got through the tunnels.

Marylebone station was a major London terminal. During the day there were lots of comings and goings, with each platform very busy. But this was a Sunday night. The only activity was the exit of the newspaper train. There

We backed up on to the train and set off on our journey

was no station pilot engine on hand. If there had been we could have left our engine and used that. The refreshment room was closed and there was a limited number of staff. The lighting was dimmed, and only one platform was in use.

There were hurried discussions with the night station staff. We swiftly explained the situation. They told us that the man who operated the hopper was at home, presumably in bed, and he had the key. They found the man's address. He did not have a telephone – very few householders had telephones – so one of their number was dispatched to his house to fetch him and the key. We didn't know how far away he lived or how he would get to the station, but in the event it was an hour before he turned up. We were so pleased to see him, and were surprised at his good nature as he had been woken up in the middle of the night. He soon filled our tender with coal. The hopper was full. He had purposely filled it at the end of his shift ready for the next time it was needed.

In the usual way, in order to generate steam in the boiler a 'steam riser' was employed at the loco sheds. It was his job to light the fires in the fireboxes in the various engines and raise steam sufficiently to enable the footplate crews to take over when they came on duty. The steam riser would lay several wooden firelighters in the firebox. These were four sticks wired together with the centre filled with creosoted wood shavings. Several firelighters would be placed in the firebox with some small coal on the top. This was then lit with a match; the fire would gradually take hold and increase until there was a large mound of burning coal. In this way the steam riser would raise steam from an engine that was cold, but our engine was warm so our situation should have been better, but it wasn't. We had no firelighters.

I knew then that I had to do something. While we were waiting for the man with the key I frantically looked for bits of wood to put in the firebox. There was no one to help me. It was the middle of the night and as the station precincts were only dimly lit I could not see properly. I stumbled over lines and sleepers and groped for bits of wood lying between the sleepers around the station yards (I even found half a sleeper) and on what appeared to me in the dark to be piles of rubbish. Eventually I found enough wood to get the fire started. I gathered it up and placed it on the platform but I knew that we still needed paper to light the fire. There was enough pressure in the boiler to get us back from the hopper to the newspaper vans on the platform. We had only 50 psi left. We just managed it.

The platform was now alive with activity. There was a hustle and bustle. The people delivering the newspapers to the train were coming and going

'Take that pile there, mate,' pointing to a pile
of the Daily Mirror

with the piles of papers that had arrived at the station. The papers were
stacked on hand trucks that were wheeled to the open doors of the train.
There were five coaches that were specifically designed to carry newspapers
and there were two ordinary coaches for passengers. The men receiving the
papers sorted out the orders for the various towns and cities and to the
distributors in the cities. They stacked them into piles ready for the waiting
trolleys at the various stations.

I started to panic. We had just managed to back up on to the train in
the platform with 50 psi in the boiler and the fire was completely out. The
daily newspapers came from London Fleet Street. The men who sorted the
newspapers ready for distribution at each station travelled up to London
Marylebone as passengers from Nottingham every night. They then loaded
up the news vans and sorted the allocations to the stations as they travelled
back to Nottingham Victoria.

I ran down the platform looking for someone to speak to. I chose the
second van as I saw someone close to the door. I shouted, 'Hey mate! Have

I climbed down wearily from the footplate, signed off,
got on my bike and slowly pedalled home

you got any old newspapers that you don't want?' The man frowned and said, 'No, we don't have old newspapers; they are all new ones!' I said, 'Well I need some newspaper to light the fire on our engine.' He stopped what he was doing and said, 'What fire?' I don't think he realised that the locomotive had a fire to make the train move. I found myself explaining where the fire was. I said, 'The fire's gone out on the engine and we need newspaper to light it. I've got some wood, and now I need the paper.' I could see he hadn't quite taken in what I was saying even then. I raised my voice. 'The fire's gone out on the engine and we need to relight it! And you won't be going anywhere if we don't get it sorted quickly.'

'This bloke here says he needs paper to light the fire on the engine,' the man said to the other men in the van. Everybody stopped. They all looked at me. I said, 'Well, come up to the engine if you don't believe me.'

The reality of it hit them then. They turned round, looked at each other and one of them who seemed to be in charge said, 'Take that pile there, mate,' pointing to a pile of the *Daily Mirror*. I snatched it – it was already tied with string ready for delivery – and ran back to the engine.

I grabbed some newspapers, perhaps 100 or so, spread them around in the firebox and piled on the wood I had found lying around. Ernie took out his Swan Vesta matches whilst I rolled a spill from one sheet of newspaper. He lit it. I reached into the firebox and lit the paper and wood. It seemed like an age before the wood and the small coal were alight properly. This was because we had only 50 psi of steam and the blower was not working well enough to get a good draught on the fire. We had to be patient. Our departure time – 1.45a.m. – came and went. We eventually got steam up and were ready to go at 4.10a.m., two and a half hours late. My driver was very calm and phlegmatic. Taking another pinch of snuff, he said, 'Can't go until we're ready.' It was only me who rushed about in a mad panic.

In the newspaper shops and news-stands in the towns of Rugby, Leicester and Nottingham the question was asked: 'Where have the daily newspapers got to?' Workmen picking up their 'daily' on the way to work and office workers and paperboys waiting to deliver all wondered if there could have been an accident. Several thousand people were affected that day.

This was not a serious incident but one of inconvenience mostly. Yet if it had become known that it was because the fire in the firebox of the railway engine that transported the news from London had simply gone out, even in those days people would have had a job to believe it. The papers did eventually arrive, of course, but several hours later and too late for some, particularly those who took the *Daily Mirror*!

When I tell this story to a group I usually finish by putting my hand in my pocket to find a box of Swan Vesta and I sum up like this: 'This is the match that lit the sticks that burned the coal that raised the steam that powered the engine that pulled the train that carried the papers clickety clack to deliver the news along the track to towns and cities there and back.'

When we finally got to Leicester I climbed down wearily from the footplate, signed off, got on my bike and slowly pedalled home.

5

JIGSAWS

It was January. The engine we had was a B1 mixed traffic engine, number 61298, and it was fairly new. Albert and I had booked on duty to work the newspaper train from Leicester Central to Nottingham Victoria on the train's last leg of its journey from London, stopping at Arkwright Street station, Nottingham and terminating at Nottingham Victoria, a mile or so further on. We travelled to the station with the locomotive ready to take the train forward. It duly arrived and we backed on to the train. The train had been brought to Leicester by a Leicester crew and in due course we left for Nottingham, after the Leicester quota of newspapers had been unloaded. It was a light train of seven coaches made up of five news vans and just two passenger coaches.

It was snowing slightly. The train was reputed to be one of the fastest in the world, from start to stop, over a short distance. It was said that sometimes it reached Nottingham Arkwright Street in nineteen and a half minutes – a distance of 23 miles. The train had to be through Loughborough in nine and a half minutes to achieve this, bearing in mind that it was uphill from Leicester to Rothley. That part of the trip passed uneventfully and having dispatched the newspapers at Arkwright Street, we made our way through the tunnel to Nottingham Victoria, where the train terminated.

By this time the snow was falling quite heavily. We uncoupled the engine, made our way onto the turntable, cleaned the fire on the ash pit, filled the tank and got coal down – that meant climbing on top of the tender and shovelling coal forward from the back of the tender ready for our return journey. We then backed up to the coaches and empty news vans, which had

We left on our return journey from
Nottingham Victoria at 6.25 a.m.

been assembled on the platform ready for their return journey to London. Other coaches and mail vans had been added to the news vans, making a total of eleven coaches. We left on our return journey from Nottingham Victoria at 6.25a.m., stopping at all stations to Leicester and beyond. We would normally have taken the train as far as Woodford Halse in Northamptonshire. By this time the snow was settling. We left on time and picked up passengers from the various stations along the way. The snow continued to fall and at times, when we were changing direction, it was difficult to see the track ahead. The snow was blinding our vision.

We arrived at Belgrave and Birstall station with no let-up in the weather. It was still dark. We drew alongside the signal box at the end of the station platform. The signalman was at his window waiting for us. He seemed very

The signalman came to his window and said all the telephone wires were down

agitated as he shouted, 'I've had no communication with Leicester passenger north signal box. I bet all the telephone wires are down because of the snow.' The last train, a goods train, had passed through his section two and a half hours before. 'Proceed forward under absolute block regulation, rule 127 section 23. Ignore all signals and be prepared to stop at any obstruction between here and Leicester passenger north.' This meant that we could take as long as we liked between these two points, as long as we didn't hit any obstruction. We left Belgrave and Birstall station with these instructions in mind and after applying steam to get the train out of the station, Albert shut the regulator as the line into Leicester is slightly downhill. We passed Abbey Lane sidings and crossed the road bridge on to St Margaret's pasture and gradually approached the viaduct.

The track was on a curve slightly to the right as it passed over St Margaret's pasture so I was first to see any obstruction from my side of the engine. I was squinting, as it was very difficult to see through the snow. I dared not take my eyes off the track. Then through this mixture of poor light and driving snow three tiny red specks appeared. I screamed at Albert, 'There's one in front, Albert!' The engine was blowing off steam. I quickly moved to put the right-hand injector on and then resumed my lookout. The three red lights were the brake lights of the stationary goods train. I yelled at Albert again at the top of my voice, 'The brakes, the brakes!' He was leaning right outside of the cab window, trying to see ahead, but because of the length of the boiler of the engine and the fact that we were on a curve he could not see the tail lights of the guard's brake ahead. The snow was blinding both of us and he did not apply the brake until he himself finally saw the guard's brake. In the meantime, I kicked the fire door trap shut as I could see the danger of a blowback happening. I knew right away that we were not going to stop.

Making a split-second decision not to jump, I wrapped my arms around the window stanchion, braced myself and waited for the inevitable. We might have toppled over the parapet; the steam pipes could have burst and we could have been badly scalded; in fact, anything could have happened. My decision to hold on and hope for the best was, I think, correct. I could not see the ground because of the snow so anything could have been underneath and furthermore it wasn't quite light. After Albert had applied the brake I felt that the train was sliding forward with its own weight. We became part of the proceedings, crashing into the train and being carried forward by the momentum until it had expended itself by smashing into four or five wagons.

The snowfall was so dense that it was difficult to assess our speed on impact, but it was probably 10–15mph at a very rough guess. By this time we were right in the centre of the viaduct – with a drop of 40–50ft either side. Our engine hit the guard's brake with an almighty bang. The engine reared up momentarily and the buffer beams sheered off, flinging one of them over the parapet. The front bogey wheels did drop back squarely on to the track but the weight of our train carried us forward, pushing the guard's brake and mangling five wagons in its wake before coming to a grinding halt. Once we had hit the guard's van we started crunching forward, smashing timbers in front of us, spewing them across the rails. I wondered whether we were going to stop, but we did. A few seconds seemed a long time.

There were thousands and thousands of jigsaw puzzles
scattered all over this white blanket of snow

I climbed gingerly down from the footplate, feeling lucky to be alive. By this time it was becoming daylight and the whole scene took on a rather surreal atmosphere. There was silence, apart from a gentle hiss of steam from the valve gear and pistons. I was knee-deep in snow. There were broken timbers and wagon wheels upended all over the track, spread over both the up and down main lines. And the most bizarre thing was that there were thousands and thousands of jigsaw puzzle pieces scattered all over this white blanket of snow. These came from boxes of jigsaw puzzles that were being transported in the wagons of the train that we had smashed into. They lay on the snow like a jigsaw carpet.

When I think of it all, I have two main recollections. One is a picture of thousands of scattered jigsaw puzzle pieces and the other is the silence after the banging and crashing of wagon wheels, the broken timber flying in the air and landing on the rails, the snow ceasing to fall, the daylight arriving and a sort of calmness extending over it all.

The first person on the scene was the guard from the goods train. His train had been held outside the station. It seems that during a shunting operation involving coaches – the station staff were assembling a passenger train in the sidings – and due to the heavy fall of snow, the points controlling one line from the next became jammed with snow and ice so they were not closing properly. One of the coaches had jumped the rail and this had prevented the goods train from passing through the station precincts. That is why it was stationary in front of us. The guard must have seen our train approaching and jumped from his guard's van and run as quickly as he could back along his own train before we hit it. Visibly shaken, he asked me if I had heard the detonators he had put down to protect his train. I hadn't heard any detonators.

After I had taken stock of the situation I stumbled back through the knee-deep snow to speak to the guard of our train. He, of course, could see what had happened. After he had checked the welfare of the passengers I assisted him in helping them down from the carriages. The drop from the carriage to the ground was about 5ft. The guard ushered all the people to one end of the coaches so that they could all get down at the same spot. There was a vertical handrail and two steps that were not normally used by passengers; they were for the use of station staff. In this emergency we used these to help the passengers scramble down. It was daylight by then. As they were led through the snow they clambered over smashed wagons that were lying across the tracks. It was 500 yards or so to the station, passing the end of the parapet.

Some of the passengers were standing when we collided with the goods train as they were anticipating alighting at Leicester Central station within a couple of minutes, so they were lucky not to get hurt. They were badly shaken but only one passenger was injured and only slightly – he had hit his head on impact.

There was an internal inquiry. The details of the incident were examined. Nobody mentioned the jigsaws. They did appreciate the difficulties we had had in getting the passengers to safety. Albert and I were both still in shock even though it was a few weeks later. We were very grateful that no one had been seriously hurt.

6

'I BET THAT BLOODY GUARD'S ASLEEP!'

Harold my driver had been a maxim gunner in the First World War. Sometimes, when we were anchored down in a siding somewhere, he would tell me stories about his time in the army in France. He had been in one of three machine-gun crews strategically placed on the battlefield with his gun weaving side to side between the crossfire of the other two guns, pointing at the advancing Germans. 'Wave after wave came at us. No one ever reached us. All killed, soldiers virtually cut in half as they charged. The gun was water-cooled and it used to boil when it was being fired constantly,' he said. I asked Harold if he had ever been scared. 'Tense, rather than scared, waiting for the signal to start firing. After the rum bottle had been passed around we did what we had to do.'

Harold was my driver on the autumn evening that we booked on duty at the Great Northern loco sheds in Syston Street, Leicester, at 8.40p.m. to take a goods train to Colwick in Nottinghamshire. Unlike the Great Central and the Midland lines which were 'through' stations, the Great Northern line terminated in Leicester. The last station before the one in Belgrave Road was Humberstone station – the scene of my story (see map in chapter 15).

We had a little B engine O6O wheel arrangement. It was a wet steam engine. That meant the steam wasn't superheated. The engine was pre-1900 with a boiler pressure of 150 psi. After an amalgamation between the Great Northern Railway and the Great Central Railway, the engines shedded at Leicester Great Northern loco in Syston Street, Leicester, were maintained by the staff of the Motive Power Department of the Great Central Locomotive Department at Leicester.

'Wave after wave came at us.
No one ever reached us'

Steam engines were still being built in the 1950s and these were superheated, operating at 225–250lb per square inch working pressure, but our little B engine had 150lb per square inch boiler working pressure.

And we had a maximum load on for that engine. The train was 'loose-coupled', which meant that the only operational brakes were the engine, tender and the guard's. Each wagon had its individual brake which was manually applied and used if the wagon was detached from the train and maybe shunted into a siding to stop it moving. Wagons in a loose-coupled train were connected to a neighbouring wagon by a loose chain coupling. Great care had to be taken when gathering the train together. It is rather like towing a car with a tow rope – you must keep the rope taut and avoid 'snatching' the rope, otherwise it could break. Railway wagons do the same. On a coal train of, say, thirty wagons, if you snatch any one of those couplings hard enough they will snap, as easy as snapping a carrot or a stick of celery. The driver must frequently look back at his wagons if he has a loose-coupled train to make sure that the train is following. The guard also had his part to play: he had to use his brake carefully and know when to apply the brake to assist the driver when coming to a stop. Whilst moving along the driver had to take note of the various gradients, gradually gathering his train. It was part of his skill. It was quite an art. The fireman had to know his job as well. An experienced fireman would know the different routes, gradients and obscure signals to look out for and when and when not to fire the engine. He would also know how to keep the water in the boiler at the proper level – not too full and certainly not too low – without being prompted by the driver. The crew relied on a green light at night and a flag in the daytime, with a 'pop pop' on the whistle to acknowledge each other and say that the train was moving along in one long chain.

The techniques of driving a loose-coupled train are quite different from driving a vacuum piped train – passenger or goods. For instance, you have to think about stopping much further in advance when you have a train with no continuous brake. A continuous brake, as on a vacuum piped system, acts on each wheel of the train, making it much more efficient.

This particular night it was autumn and the leaves were falling, covering the lines. This made the lines slippery. It was so important that at this time of the year the sand in the sandboxes moved freely in case we were required to force it under the driving wheels in order to give us adhesion. It was also important that the lubricator was working properly and a regular supply of oil was reaching the valves and pistons. Frequent checks were necessary on the sight glass of the lubricator to make sure that the oil was flowing properly.

The lubricator was mounted on the framing and the sight glass was usually mounted on the faceplate on the fireman's side. The lubricator was adjustable so that when the engine was working hard you could increase the oil supply accordingly. The lubricators on later engines were regulated automatically. That night, although the sandboxes were full, the sand was damp and did not run freely through the pipes. It was a steep incline straight from the sidings and on to the main line and the engine began to slip as we took load. The sandboxes containing the sand that I needed were fitted on the framing above the driving wheels. The pipes on this engine were mounted immediately in front of the driving wheels and the sand was oscillated via a linkage of rods to a handle on the footplate. I rocked this sand handle backwards and forwards but no sand came through the pipes. I suggested to Harold that I threw some ballast under the driving wheels.

So, as we were moving at barely a walking pace, I climbed down and walked along with the engine and threw shovelfuls of ballast (ballast was used to support sleepers) under the driving wheels to lend adhesion. I did this for maybe a quarter of a mile. As soon as the wheels started to grip and we picked up speed, I hopped back on board and slowly we were on our way. We duly arrived at Colwick with our train. I uncoupled the wagons from the engine and we went to the loco sheds, coaled up, watered, cleaned the fire and made our way back to the marshalling yards ready to take another train back to Leicester. We left Colwick around 5.30a.m. with a mixed train of coal and goods wagons. The incline up which we had struggled a few hours before now became the reverse. This time we had to hold the train back. The engine and the tender brakes were the only way to do this. It was the guard's job to drag his brake to assist us in slowing the train down as we went down the incline, but of course we had no way of knowing whether this was happening as we had no communication with him.

As the track was all downhill from Thurnby station we shut off steam well before the distant signal for Humberstone station came into view. The signal was against us. We anticipated the home signal to be against us too, which indeed it was. A further home signal, the inner one that guarded Forest Road crossing gates, was also against us.

I applied the tender brake whilst Harold applied the steam brake – the usual procedure with a loose-coupled train. It didn't seem to make much difference to our speed as we passed the distant signal and went on towards the stop signals at Humberstone station. Although we were taking steps to control the train, we could tell that we were being pushed down the gradient by the sheer weight of the wagons. The track towards Humberstone station and the crossing gates was on a slight curve and the early morning sun made everything look bright – a perfect picture with the signals, the station, the crossing gates and the people all encapsulated momentarily as we got closer and closer. That's when we began to panic as the enormity of the situation dawned. Normally the crossing gates would be closed to traffic to allow the train – our train – to pass into the marshalling yards which were a few hundred yards further on; we had had a clear passage all week. But on this day, a Thursday, because the siding we were scheduled to run into in the marshalling yard had not been cleared ready for us by the shunters, the signalman at Humberstone station who controlled the crossing gates had to hold us until the station yard staff had cleared the siding.

I had to move very quickly. We slid through Humberstone station, passing the stop boards. We were not in control of the train; it was controlling us. We had the full weight of the wagons, amounting to many tons, pushing us downhill on an already slippery line.

Our brakes were full on and it became obvious that we were going too fast to stop at the home signal guarding the crossing. Harold wrenched the reversing lever into back gear and applied full steam. In our desperate efforts to bring the train to a standstill the wheels on this little B engine began to

I grabbed the coal hammer, jumped down from the engine and ran along beside the wagons

*I spragged the brakes down with the shaft of
the coal hammer on the wagons as they passed me*

churn backwards and the sparks were flying. I yelled, 'I'll sprag the brakes on
the wagons!'

I grabbed the coal hammer, jumped down from the engine and ran along
beside the wagons. I spragged the brakes down with the shaft of the coal
hammer on the wagons as they passed me, so the wheels on each wagon

We stopped 2ft from the gates

became locked and began to skid along the track. This added more braking power to the train. Nearer and nearer we moved towards the crossing gates. After spragging five of the wagons I knew I had to get back on to the footplate because the train was beginning to pass me. I ran after the engine, tripping over sleepers and slippery ballast, and finally climbed back on board. I looked to see if there was anything else I could do to help us stop, as well as making sure that we still had plenty of steam and water in the boiler as I had left these duties temporarily to themselves. It was a case of hoping for the best as we had done everything we possibly could to bring the train to a standstill. It was then that I looked out at the gates. People's expressions had turned from mild curiosity to horror as we slid towards them. But they didn't run away, they appeared to be transfixed! There must have been fifteen or twenty people walking across the crossing, some just going to work on that morning, some pushing prams, others walking their bicycles. The local coalman had his horse and cart, and one man was even leaning over the crossing gate smoking his pipe as if he was passing the time of day. But Harold's experience and my spragging of the wagons were beginning to do the trick. We stopped 2ft from the gates.

The signalman did not report us for passing the stop boards – he could see what we were having to do in order to stop.

After we finally came to a grinding halt Harold and I looked at each other with a sigh of relief. 'I bet that bloody guard was asleep,' Harold said. We also both suspected that we had rather more tonnage to pull than we should have had for the size of the engine. Harold patted me on the shoulder. 'Great stuff, mate,' he said.

And one man was even leaning over the crossing gate smoking his pipe

1

'PUT THE KETTLE ON AND SHOUT UP THE STAIRS!'

The church clock struck three. There was no one around. Any sound was muffled by heavy snow. It had covered the glass of the street lamps so they were giving off very little light. I stood on the traffic island inside the estate, about a quarter of a mile off the main road. I walked round it several times trying to find the road signs. The snow was knee-deep by this time and had blown up against them. There were four exits and I couldn't find the one I wanted. In any case, I had by now lost any sense of direction. I didn't know where I had come from or which way I should go. I was lost!

I stood there stamping my feet to keep warm. I thought that if I stayed on the island someone was bound to come along and show me the way back to the main road and then I would know where I was. I had heard the clock strike and that meant I was at least an hour late.

After what seemed like an age a man appeared in front of me. The shoulders of his dark overcoat and his hat were white with the falling snow. He was, he said, a postman on his way to work. He pointed in the direction of the main road.

I was the 'knocker up' that night. At the start of my career on the railway, after six months' cleaning engines and doing odd jobs round the loco sheds, the running foreman had called me to the office and asked me if I knew Leicester well since a knocker up was needed for the night shift the following week. I said I knew it pretty well as I had lived there all my life. So that was settled. I reported for duty at midnight on Sunday for knocking up duties.

It was the duty of the knocker up to go round the homes of the drivers and firemen to wake them an hour before they were due to book on duty. This

He pointed in the direction of the main road

*He said, handing me the fish slice, 'Have a
go whilst I make the tea'*

applied between the hours of twelve o'clock at night and seven o'clock in the
morning. Our depot had only one knocker up, but others had a team. This
depended on the number of loco men.

It was assumed that I could ride a bike and I was presented with a list of
the addresses of the loco men with certain instructions for some of them,
such as 'line prop at back of dustbin', 'tap hard on window', 'don't knock
too loud', 'knock if curtains are closed', 'shout through the letterbox', 'back
door will be open', 'put kettle on the gas and shout up the stairs' and so on.
I set off and made my first call to a fireman who lived at a fish and chip shop
and who I had happened to see just a few days before I took the job. He had
said, 'Come round early and I'll get you some tea.' I reached the shop about
one o'clock. I knocked and he opened the door brandishing a fish slice,
saying, 'Come in, I've just been killing a few.' When I got inside the shop
I noticed that the walls appeared to be moving on either side of the range.
Then I realised that it wasn't the walls that were moving but thousands of
cockroaches. Apparently they came out at night when the range was shut
down. 'No sign of any in the day,' the fireman said, handing me the fish slice.
'Have a go whilst I make the tea.'

I was the 'knocker up' that night

The church clock struck three

My next call at 2.15 was in the red light area. Talk about an embarrassing moment or two! In order to get to the house I had to go down a long dark entry. It turned out to be a favourite spot for the ladies of the night to congregate. I couldn't tell how many people were in the entry but it appeared to be quite crowded. I stood my bike up against a lamppost and started to walk up the entry. I had my lamp with me, but didn't switch it on, somehow thinking it wasn't quite appropriate. First, I came across two people. I simply could not get by them and stood there wondering what to do. Then, as predicted, after a minute or two they muttered things that I am sure were not very complimentary and then let me pass. I walked further up the entry, wondering what other treats were in store, but there was another couple who were just discussing financial arrangements, so I was able to make my call. I tapped on the window with the line prop as instructed. I was a bit worried that I was going to break the window, but the bedroom light came on and a hand waved down to acknowledge my knock. When I returned to my bike, thinking I would have to run the gauntlet again, there was no sign of anyone. They had just disappeared into the night.

My next calls were on a council estate about 2 miles further across Leicester. By this time the snow was falling quite heavily. I was just able to ride the railway bike but it was becoming increasingly difficult. Not long afterwards it became impossible. It was a struggle even to push it, so I decided to lean it against the fence of someone's house and continue on foot. It was here that I heard the clock strike three.

A search party was sent out the next day to retrieve the bike. It was still where I had left it. I had had to leave it with calls not made and tramp back to the loco shed to tell my sorry tale to the foreman who had sent me out in the first place. He was sympathetic and sent me home. I slept for ten hours.

This was about four months before I relinquished the job of knocker up and got my first firing job. In that time I gradually got to know where I had to go. I had my own ports of call for cups of tea. The council used to employ nightwatchmen and their duties were to make sure that the red light warning lamps were lit around a road works. They were paraffin lamps that had to be lit at dusk and kept alight until daylight the next morning. Their general duty was to keep an eye on things and make sure that the equipment that had to

It became impossible to ride the bike any further

be left on the site overnight was safe. They would have a portable canvas hut to sit in and always had the kettle boiling. I passed these road works on the way to my last calls of the night. The nightwatchman said he was glad of my company. He was nervous as a fellow nightwatchman had been murdered on a site in the town a few days before. I often sat with him, chatting and dozing before his coke-filled brazier. As I left him to make my last call the dawn chorus and the new day gave him reassurance.

The council used to employ nightwatchmen

8

LINE OF PROMOTION

'**So you shovelled** coal, did you? Like on the *Titanic?*'

I was having drinks in a friend's garden. It was midsummer. I was surprised to learn that my friend had never travelled on a steam train even though he had lived in England in the 1950s. I explained what I did for a living at that time, which prompted me to tell him how it was that I came to get started.

'Did you want to be a driver?' he asked. 'Or did you want just to be a fireman?'

'No, I could not be just a fireman,' I replied. 'You were a midshipman but that didn't mean you would automatically become an Admiral! A police constable does not always progress to be the chief constable! If you enrol as a nurse it doesn't necessarily mean you will become the matron. But being employed by the railway as a future footplate man is quite different. Here there is automatic promotion, so the answer to your question is that I knew I would be a driver – sometime. Equally, I did not have the choice to stop where I was as a cleaner, or as a fireman. The promotion ladder relentlessly allowed progress. Other people have asked me the same question.'

I then explained what was termed the Line of Promotion. I held up my hand, extending five fingers.

'There are five rungs on the promotion ladder. To become a fast train driver you would have to take this route: at the age of 16 or above and after a check on your health and eyesight you would be employed in the locomotive department as an engine cleaner. This is the first rung on the ladder.'

'So you shovelled coal, did you? Like on the *Titanic*?'

'After several months you would sit an exam to ensure you knew the duties of a fireman and were familiar with the Rule Book. If you passed this satisfactorily you were regarded as eligible to perform light firing duties, which would be on shunting engines in the marshalling yards or on the occasional local goods train to outlying districts. This is the second rung of the ladder. You were then a passed cleaner/spare fireman. The time from being a passed cleaner to being a registered fireman could often be a lengthy one because you were waiting for a vacancy.

'The third rung of the ladder would be as a registered fireman. This could not happen until an express train driver, who was usually at the very top of the list, took retirement. Then everyone moved up. A position on the promotion list depended entirely on the date on which you were first employed by the company in the locomotive department. It was possible to be senior on this list to men older than yourself as there were men being demobbed from the armed forces at that time.

'The fourth step was as a passed fireman/spare driver. This meant passing the appropriate exams. You would eventually become a regular driver and ultimately one that drives fast trains – the fifth and final rung of the promotion ladder. This applied to fast train and mixed traffic depots, but not to goods depots as there were no fast trains there.

'The reality of the job was that if work was lost, possibly having been allocated to another depot or to different routes, there would not be sufficient work for all the drivers on the registered list. Drivers, therefore, often had to work as firemen or apply for posts at other depots to maintain their driver status. If, however, the depot was given extra work, the opposite happened.'

Some people satisfy their childhood dreams by building a miniature railway in their garden. To others the fascination of the steam locomotive belching flames and smoke is satisfied by images obtained through poetry and painting. Trainspotters, too, have their enthusiasms. In this lovely summer garden I watched the interest of my friend increase. As I sat down with another lager I told him the story about the night in the mid-1950s when the fire went out (chapter 4), when I was on stage three of the promotion ladder.

Pressed to describe even more, I thought I would tell my friend about the conditions on the footplate itself which change their nature as the engine gets into its stride. It is a bit like a ship on the sea. When a ship leaves harbour it meets weather changes. I was fascinated by the change from standing dormant to experiencing 150 tons of steel jumping around at high speed. The faster the engine travelled, the louder the sounds became, until a certain speed was reached and the noise level seemed to remain constant.

B1 steam locomotive faceplate

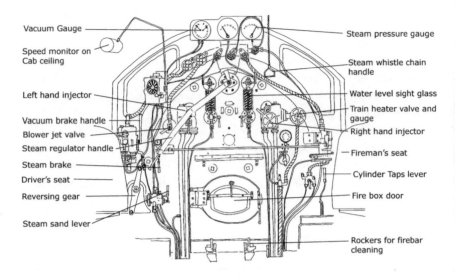

Vacuum Gauge

Speed monitor on Cab ceiling

Left hand injector

Vacuum brake handle
Blower jet valve
Steam regulator handle

Steam brake

Driver's seat

Reversing gear

Steam sand lever

Steam pressure gauge

Steam whistle chain handle

Water level sight glass

Train heater valve and gauge

Right hand injector

Fireman's seat

Cylinder Taps lever

Fire box door

Rockers for firebar cleaning

NOT TO SCALE some pipe lines and fittings have been omitted

When I was going to work on a Pacific locomotive footplate, *Blink Bonny* for example, I knew that I had more room in which to work than I would have on a smaller engine. I would have been constantly aware that I might knock my knuckles when swinging the shovel. And the temperature in the cab of a Pacific was hotter than a goods engine, because the Pacific cab was almost entirely enclosed. As far as speaking to my colleague was concerned, very little conversation occurred while we were travelling along. We used hand gestures so that we did not have to cross the footplate to shout into each other's ears. The noise in the cab was caused by a combination of sounds: the swaying and jolting of the engine (especially if the engine was the worse for wear); the bark from the chimney as the engine was asking for more; the blast from the firebox; and the valves and pistons going backwards and forwards. If you were required to work an engine that you had not fired before, you were actually entering a new workplace. It was necessary to adapt quickly to the different engines' designs. On top of that, sometimes the driver's controls were on the right side of the footplate rather than on the customary left.

After explaining all of this to my friend I mentioned my burgeoning interest in keeping chickens and, as the shadows began to get longer, the afternoon ended with a guided tour around his chicken coops.

9

EXTRA-CURRICULAR

In common with other railwaymen, I spent some of my spare time earning extra money. The shift system encouraged me. The spare time during the day and a need to save towards a deposit on a house pushed me towards window cleaning, chimney sweeping and even selling Turkey red handkerchiefs! This chapter includes tales about the first two and adds one or two thoughts about my life at that time, all of which in some way I thank the railway for!

Ad verbatim!

Right. A friend and I had a talk in the pub about doing some spare-time work. We thought that chimney sweeping might not be a bad bet. So I went down to the hardware shop in Leicester, that shop that all Leicester people knew, and I bought a sweep set. It cost £2 10s. I brought it home and we had a little talk. We decided to charge 3s 6d a chimney. We needed a bag to put up against the chimney breasts to collect the soot that was going to come down the chimneys when we swept them. So we made one (a bag) out of an old sheet. My grandmother suggested we cut a hole in it and sew an arm of a shirt on it so that when you put the brushes up, it kept the soot inside the bag.

We were anxious to get started but needed to have a practice. So this is what we did and also where we made a mistake. We chose a chimney with no soot in it. We decided to have a go at our front room chimney – it had never

We thought that chimney sweeping might not be a bad bet!

had a fire in it. We didn't use the living room chimney because it was in daily use, and was probably very sooty as it hadn't been swept for some time. We pushed the brush up, straight out the top, pulled it back, no problems. So we thought, that's it, we're in business.

The first chimney we did was that of my friend's future mother-in-law. We arrived there in the early afternoon, put the bag up, set everything out so we didn't get soot all over the place and started to push the brush up the chimney. Well, everything went well until we got about three-quarters of the way up the chimney, but then the going got tough because as much as we tried to push the rods up, they wouldn't go. Nothing would go. The rods were bending all shapes and although we really tried to push them up they refused, so we decided to put the scraper up. We brought the brushes down and to our horror found the brush had gone. We told the lady of the house that we simply had to put the scraper up; we didn't dare tell her we had lost the brush. So up went the scraper and we still couldn't get through to the top of the chimney. The lady said she thought we were doing a very good job and we kept sending her out to see if the scraper had come out of the top so that we could talk. We sent her up the garden so she could watch for it. 'The usual sweep only takes ten minutes or so to sweep the chimney,' she said, and we had been there for an hour and a half so she concluded that 'usual sweeps don't really do the job properly'. We knew that we had got to announce that we had lost the brush. But we had a plan. We said that we had lost it but before she had a chance to reply we asked if she knew where we could borrow a ladder from because we thought the brush was lodged in the pot at the top. She picked up on the urgency in our voices. 'The television people just across the road will lend you a ladder.' So without more ado we ran across and borrowed their big double ladder. We put the ladder up to the slates. I ran back home to put my baseball boots on, came back, shinned up the ladder and when I got to the slates on the roof I could see that I still had to go further up the slates to the apex of the roof to the chimney stack. Also, the chimney stack was higher than I thought; it didn't look much when you were looking up from the ground but it was really quite high. And then on top of that there was at least another 3ft to the top of the chimney pot. Meanwhile, a crowd had gathered in the garden: the bread man, the milkman and several neighbours and the children who had just come out of school. They were all looking up. It was then about four o'clock and just getting dark. I was thankful when people started shouting 'come down and leave it till tomorrow'. I didn't need to be told twice. I hadn't even got a crawl ladder. I came down.

The circumstances then meant the lady was not able to have a fire that evening. Her husband was a building worker and he, we understood, had been a bit apprehensive about letting us do the job in the first place. He came home about quarter past four and there was no fire in the grate and they had to sit round a one bar electric until the next day. It was quite a big family – about nine of them.

We arrived promptly the next day. It was one o'clock when we had finished our railway shifts. We started earnestly with the scraper to try to pull the missing brush down, but unfortunately to no avail. So between us we decided that we had to go into the rafters of the house to the chimney flue to locate the brush. Time was getting short as this was the middle of winter and it got dark at about four o'clock. We used a pair of steps and got up into the rafters. We hadn't got a light of any sort; we had two candles and a scraper and a hammer. We had to be careful as we walked along the rafters in case we put our feet through the ceiling. Things were quite desperate. As soon as we got to the chimney flues – there were four – we started pulling out the bricks. Fortunately, the mortar was very soft but we in our enthusiasm got into the wrong flue – we were in the bedroom flue. When we realised it we got into the next one which was the right one. We started feverishly to pull out the bricks. There was a large gaping hole in the chimney breast. I pushed my arm through and reached up into the soot and hey presto, there was the brush. 'Thank God,' we shouted down, 'we've found it!' Then began the job of putting the bricks back. We asked whether the lady had any cement and sand. She had a tiny bit, so we mixed the sand and cement together on the dustbin lid. We really needed quite a bit more cement, but we did what we could. Now, the skylight was rectangular, so when it came to going up the steps with the dustbin lid full of sand and cement mixture we had to tip it slightly in order to get through the opening. That was when a large quantity of cement slipped off the dustbin lid and fell on to the stairs' carpet. Eventually we got it through and proceeded to put the bricks back. We ran out of cement entirely and finished up packing the bricks with wet sand to fill the joints. Job done. We just managed to get down the ladder, clean up and get a fire going in the grate before the lady's husband burst in the back door. His first words were, 'Have they done it?' and his wife was beaming as she said, 'Yes.'

'We would have you again,' was her parting shot to us when her husband had gone for a wash. 'When you've had a bit more practice,' she added quietly.

The wedding present

A friend, a fellow railway fireman, had just got married and said he would like us to sweep his chimney. We like to think he had heard how good we were! He had just moved into an old cottage in the town. Because he couldn't be there when we were to sweep the chimney he was to leave the keys under a brick outside the back door.

We arrived in the early afternoon. We set up our kit around the fireplace, taking care to move everything that was on the mantelpiece to the sideboard before we started. In recent weeks we had made a slight modification to the sweep set. In case the brush came off in the chimney, and as an extra precaution, we had screwed a clothesline to the brush. It had appeared a bit loose when we assembled the rods.

After we had put the bag up against the fireplace we connected the rods to each other, gradually pushing them up the chimney. After six rods had gone up I noticed that the clothesline wasn't going up the chimney, which was rather strange as it was attached to the brush. So we decided to bring everything back down to see what had happened. All that came down were the rods, without the brush. The brush was still up the chimney. And worse! When we counted the rods, there was a rod missing. So Plan B had to come into operation.

Plan B consisted of a pull on the clothesline (which was attached to the brush). Surely that was all that was needed? But alas, when we pulled on the clothesline it wouldn't come down. Here we were, with a rod missing, the brush missing and the clothesline mysteriously stuck up the chimney. Daylight was going and we had to switch the light on.

It was obvious that what we had to do was put the scraper up and try to dislodge the brush. Easy! We attached the scraper to the rods and pushed the lot up the chimney. This is where the slight panic set in. I could tell we had gone too far up. It was then that my friend said, 'I can feel it. I can feel it.' He was pulling hard on the rods when, suddenly, there was a knock on the kitchen door. I opened the door and looked down. There stood a little boy. He was pointing upwards. 'Ooh mister, ooh mister mister,' he said. 'There's all bricks and mortar coming down from your roof.' We dashed outside and looked up. To our horror the chimney pot was on its side, trapping the scraper. This was preventing us from pulling the rods down the chimney, which we had been trying to do.

We had lost the brush and one rod, the scraper was trapped by the chimney pot and it was getting dark.

We happened to know a builder whose yard, attached to his house, was nearby. We ran round, knocked on the door and asked if he had a ladder we could borrow. He had just one, a very long one. We explained our immediate predicament. We gave him a garbled account of what had happened and he said we could borrow the ladder. Time was against us. The ladder was hanging on the wall. We took it and ran back down the street, my friend at the front end of the ladder and myself at the rear. By now it was 5p.m. People were knocking off. When we came to the main road I had to run wide in order to get round the corner and across the road. We didn't stop for the traffic, we gambled that it would stop for us. Just as I got round the corner I noticed a man spinning round and round. He was holding his face. We didn't stop; we just kept on running until we got back to our friend's cottage. I said, 'Did you see the man holding his face? I think we hit him with the end of the ladder!' We didn't have time to ponder, because we needed to put the ladder up against the wall so that we could go up on to the roof to release the pot. A voice suddenly said, 'I'll do that for you.' It was the builder – he had followed us round, unbeknown to us. He could see what a mess we were in. He went straight up the ladder while we went inside the house. We pulled the scraper down as he lifted the pot upright and that, in the process, pulled the brush and the rod down as well as I gently pulled the clothesline. We managed to get all three down the chimney.

We were so grateful to the builder but didn't have time to thank him. By the time we had finished he had gone.

It was really dark now. We hadn't realised what a mess we had created. Soot was everywhere. It had settled on all the new ornaments – no doubt they were wedding presents – arranged nicely in different parts of the room. We shook the soot out of vases, eggcups, a pair of slippers that had been left out, and off the pictures on the wall. There was even soot on the new lampshade. Then we packed up our kit. Before we left the house I glanced round to see that we had replaced everything properly and noticed there were two splits in the new green lino just in front of the fireplace. The toecaps of my boots must have gone through at the spot where I had been kneeling. It seems that as it was an old cottage the floor was very uneven so the workmen who had laid the lino had packed it up with paper. Fortunately the new hearthrug, another wedding present probably, just covered the two splits. The generosity of the builder, combined with a bit of luck with the size of the hearthrug, enabled us to finish the job.

We sighed with relief. We locked the door, put the keys back under the brick and left. We didn't charge of course. We said it was a wedding present.

Eleven pounds a fortnight

One bucket.
One double twelve-rung ladder.
Two separate square yards of scrim.
One chamois leather.
And water from the first house on the round (hot or cold water, preferably hot in the winter!)

I was in business.

I had to buy the window-cleaning round. The price was the amount of money I would earn by cleaning the entire round once. This would be once a month. I gave the £11 to the retiring window cleaner with anticipation. It looked to be a good round: large palisaded three-storey Victorian houses, built to accommodate business and professional people and to give a good impression to visitors to the city. The houses were on the main road into the town. The fronts of the houses faced the road, the rear of the houses were in the next street.

My initial encounter with my customers was when I knocked on the door of the first house. The doorknocker was old and heavy. The door was opened by a middle-aged lady. I started to explain that I was the new window cleaner and that I was ready to clean the windows. She was not impressed; in fact, she glowered at me. This is exactly what she said, in a voice I can only describe as like brittle toffee: 'I don't know you.' (Pause.) 'I don't know you.' (Another pause.) 'I definitely don't know you!' Here she wagged her finger at me. I said, 'I know you don't know me,' and I repeated my polite introduction. She said: 'I don't know you.' (Pause.) 'I don't know you.' (Another pause.) 'I definitely don't know you.' Her shrill voice went up a decibel or two.

At that I said, politely, that I was sorry to have bothered her and I started to move away. But she followed me into the road, still wagging her finger, rather frighteningly for me now, shouting, 'I don't know you. I don't know you. I definitely don't know you!' Like the chorus of a song! I thought, here's one to leave out. So every time I did my round I gave her a miss.

When I was talking to her next-door neighbour, perhaps three months later, I was told more about her. I began to feel that I should reconsider the situation, as the windows were terribly dirty by this time. It was explained that I had knocked on the door to make my introductions in an afternoon and that is why I got the strange reception that I did. Apparently, I should have gone in a morning because 'she's ok in the morning and drunk in the afternoon'. This lady lived alone and her behaviour was very odd, particularly in the afternoons. It seemed that she had a habit of crawling across the main road on all fours, stopping the traffic. People had got used to the sight of her. Even the bus drivers were looking out for her. So when I first knocked on her door it was an afternoon, the worst time of her day.

A few weeks later she came to the door one morning purposely to ask me if I would clean an extra window as well as those I had already agreed to do. This was an attic window at the back of the house that could not be reached by ladder and had obviously been ignored by previous window cleaners as it was very grimy. A window cleaner would have to do what I did – sit backwards on the sill, pull the window towards him and clean it from that position. Cleaning this attic window meant I had to go inside the house. Stepping inside the house was a revelation! There was ornate furniture, a hand-carved table and dresser, chaise longue, the floors carpeted with thick carpets, heavy drapes at the windows, almost as if the house had been furnished decades earlier and time had stood still. Even though it was a morning (I had made sure of that) and the light was bright there was a sombre feel. The wallpaper was heavily embossed. Also, there was net at the windows, which filtered the light, adding to the gloom. Outside the house, in the back garden, I noticed piles of gin bottles. Once I'd cleaned the window she offered me a cup of tea, which I accepted. What did catch my eye was the painting over the mantelpiece. As I stood looking at it, the lady said, 'I believe that's a Gainsborough, my father's favourite painter.' I didn't know who her father was but I would have liked to have known. The painting was dirty, had an ornate gold leaf frame and a quality that I know is recognisable in paintings by great masters. I had been told that the lady was quite different in the mornings, and she was on this occasion. She spoke with a cultured voice as she looked at me through red-rimmed eyes.

A white linen napkin was carefully folded into a silver napkin ring and placed correctly on a white laced tablecloth that covered the table standing in the centre of the dining room. A setting for one. It was said that she always set the table in this way before she took the tram into the town where she went for her first drinks of the day. She staggered back in the early afternoon and had a solitary meal. She would have been in her afternoon gloom by then. From a weepy, quiet person two hours earlier, she became an aggressive individual, at times wielding a stick and capable of speaking to me in the way she did.

Further along the road lived an elderly couple who were customers of mine. Their back gate was always locked so I had to put my ladder up against the wall, lift it and slide it down the other side so that I could open the gate and let myself into the garden. This particular day there were two dogs in the garden. I had never seen dogs at that house before, although I had cleaned the windows several times. The dogs came bounding towards me. I like dogs, but I wasn't sure what reception I would get so I stood wondering what to do. But in my dilemma I had left the gate open. Out shot the dogs into the street. I wasn't too bothered until I had put my ladder up to the windows ready to clean them and the lady came to the door to greet me, said, 'Hello,' took one look down the garden and screamed, 'My dogs! My dogs! My prize dogs! You've let my prize dogs out.' I rushed to the gate and looked both ways up and down the street. No dogs. No sign of dogs. To the left was the main road and to the right an avenue. I didn't know which way to run but decided to go to the right. Fortunately, I had chosen the correct way. The lady called, 'Catch the young one if you can!'

I grabbed my bike and pedalled as fast as I could. There was no sign of either dog. I tried the next street. There was the older dog sitting calmly in the middle of the road. The younger one, the one I was supposed to catch, was rushing down every entry it came to. It had never had freedom like this before. The terraced houses, it had discovered, had entries but no exits. The dog was simply working its way down the street, in one entry and out again, in the next and out again. It was a long street. I left the older dog sitting in the middle of the road, pedalled down the avenue to the entry the young dog had just gone into and waited for it at the top. I grabbed him.

He licked my face. He was an Old English sheepdog and therefore was no lightweight. I sat on my bike with the wriggling dog under my arm and started to ride back to the house. All went well until we turned the corner. The dog's tail got caught in the bike spokes. It screamed in pain. The bike, the dog and I landed in the road – me at the bottom, the dog next and then the bike on top. I finally extracted its tail from the spokes and it stopped howling but I noticed there were a few tufts of hair missing – they were in the bike spokes. I was determined not to let the dog go so I walked the bike the rest of the way, carrying the struggling animal under my right arm. I was glad to hear that the older dog had eventually been persuaded to stand up and allow its owner to walk him home.

I was apprehensive on the next occasion I was booked to clean those windows. I didn't know what to expect. As I carefully closed the gates behind me both dogs saw me and came bounding up. The fact that one had a tail with a white bandage at its tip, standing up vertically, like a flagpole, did not deter it from running up to greet me and do what it had done before, lick my face. No hard feelings. I like dogs.

Day Excursion

The children held their buckets and little wooden spades and mums had the sandwiches. I don't remember any Day Excursion when the weather was bad. The sun was shining, it was midsummer and we were taking families to the coast for the day.

Leicester is in the centre of England, about 100 miles from the coast. This represents two hours on the train. Non-corridor stock was often used for Day Excursions meaning there were no toilets. This accounted for the queue of children that could be seen on the station platform as the train crew got the locomotive ready for the journey. We were to be the crew for both journeys, there and back. That meant we had six hours of spare time.

These outings were often planned months ahead, in the dark days of the winter. This was the great day. Anticipating the ride on the train was part of the pleasure; in fact, it was a large part. So to climb into a coach on a train that had smoke bellowing out of its engine was very exciting. What's more, the train made a noise, a special noise that only applied to trains. The children started to eat as soon as the train started to move.

We generally went to Skegness. It was the job of a different crew to turn the engine and prepare the train for the return journey so we had a few hours to spare. While the families enjoyed the fresh air of the east coast, as well as the sand, sea and ice cream, my driver Harold and I spent the first hour in the Lumley Bar, then we wandered round the shops, remembering to buy bright pink sticks of rock with 'Skegness' written all the way through them for our own families at home. There were stalls with shrimps, whelks and mussels, which all tasted so wonderful. We bought several bags for ourselves.

'Let's go and watch the bowling,' Harold said. We took our brown paper bags full of cockles and mussels, together with the sandwiches we had brought from home, strolled down the promenade to the bowling green and settled ourselves on a seat. There were similar seats all around the green. The bowling was held next to an area where tropical fish, special hothouse plants, seals, snakes and even crocodiles were kept.

I noticed that most of the onlookers were elderly. Some were dozing. Some were in wheelchairs. Suddenly we saw a very large rat snake wriggling across the green to where the bowlers were, all looking intensely downwards as they studied the bowls on the grass in front of them. They weren't aware of the snake at that point. One minute the atmosphere was calm on such a pleasant afternoon and the next minute there was uproar. The old people screamed with fright. The snake, which must have been

The children held their buckets and little wooden spades

6ft long, just worked its way round the bowls on the green, which was very quickly deserted. One group hid behind the toilet block and another in the sand dunes. Others ran, or were hurriedly pushed out of the way. It was ages before the keeper came to capture it. Over his shoulder he had a large net on a pole. It seems that the snake had come under the netting from the building next door. The keeper was anxious to catch it before it got to the ice cream bar on the beach. It was heading that way! He managed to corner it and get it into the net by himself. No one seemed to want to help him. We stood up when this all happened but I am ashamed to say we did nothing.

We sat on the wall at the edge of the promenade for the remainder of our spare time, watching the children have rides on the donkeys – two footplate men enjoying an ice cream each, with a bit of ras' on the top!

We struck away from Skegness in the early evening. We had come most of the way when we began to move very slowly. We knew why it was happening: the coal was bad quality, we were going uphill, and we had ten carriages full of day trippers. We had been struggling ever since we left Skegness. Normally it wasn't possible to hear anything other than footplate noises, but because we were moving so slowly I was able to hear voices. I looked back down the train and saw two little heads poking out of the first carriage window. Two little boys were waving and shouting at us. 'Can you go a bit faster, mister?' one said. It summed up our predicament. The engine had not steamed very well for some time, so the brake had automatically gone on because there was not sufficient steam to maintain the brake mechanism. We eventually stopped entirely just opposite the clock at Ingarsby station.

We were having what was called a 'blow up'. I poked the fire with the straight dart to break up the clinker that had formed on the fire bars. We hoped to raise a bit more steam, which is what happened. This just about got us to the point on the journey where, fortunately, Leicester is geographically 'downhill' – in a dip in the landscape – and was to our advantage.

Tired and a little late we all came home safely.

Football special

Our train had come from the north. We took it onwards from Leicester. It was a Saturday and we were carrying football fans from Manchester to Wembley for a big match. When a football special was involved the coaches were always full. This was no exception. We got to Wembley station in time and watched everyone alight. They were noisy and good-natured, anticipating a good match that afternoon.

One fan, an older man, approached the cab. He was a supporter; we knew that because he had a scarf in his team's colours and a northern accent. He said, 'Here you are lads, we've had a collection for you. Don't get drunk, we need you to bring us back again.' He handed me his cap full of money; half-crown pieces, sixpences, threepenny bits, pennies, all were there. After I had thanked him I put the cap carefully into the locker so that we could count the money when we got to Marylebone station. There must have been at least the amount a driver would earn in a week. We each had a third. We decided it was all a bit of northern generosity and a pleasant surprise.

Tavern in the town

I never said I didn't want to go to work. What the railway offered was hellish freedom; you booked on and you got on with it. There was a camaraderie that was special to the railway. Life outside the railway and life within it were different. Railwaymen who gathered at pubs – and not all did – asked questions like 'what shift are you on?' and as there were sixteen shifts the answers were varied. The second (and sometimes the third and the fourth) question was, 'Are you going to try one?'

Railwaymen did not tire of talking about their job; they were consumed by it. Pubs were meeting places to come back to and compare experiences. The mess room was ok, always warm, but it didn't sell beer! A pub was warm, sold beer, and the conversation did not flag. There were benches in the pub backyard. We just propped our bikes up against the wall and went inside to meet our fellow railwaymen.

One pub had a remarkable landlord and landlady. They liked a pint – or two! So much so that they were frequently semi-drunk and we had to pull our own beer and put the money into the till. The landlord was always talking about his time in the army, when apparently he spent time in Benghazi. We all knew these tales and we all knew the name Benghazi. We said it like this – Bengaaahzee – when he wasn't listening.

This pub was very old. It had an air about it as soon as you went in. I suppose it was a combination of all the years when beer, wine and spirits had been sold and pipe and cigarette smoke. It had sort of pickled the place; got into the walls. This all added to the aroma that met you as you opened the door.

In the winter, well most of the year, there was an open fire to greet you. The landlord's dog would be sprawled across the hearth seemingly asleep, but actually listening for the crackle of crisp packets. As soon as a packet was opened his ear would go up and he would stagger towards you expectantly. It was a pub where local traders would call in on their rounds for 'a quick one'. Towards dinnertime the friendly banter became a general hubbub. Deals were arranged in there; there was trading. A couple of rabbits would be brought in for sale. Bets were passed to the bookies runner 'under the table' as it was illegal to gamble in a pub. The local fishmonger would come in with a load of sprats. The smell of his apron and the sprats lingered for quite a while after he had gone. Two old ladies met there every day. They had half a pint each and made their drinks last for at least two hours. The landlord, with his dry humour, murmured, 'I won't get rich from that pair!' Very often there was a domino school going on – sometimes with rail men or sometimes just the locals and as you sat there staring into the fire, listening to a tale or two from your mates, time seemed to stand still. It was only when your conscience told you it was time to go home that you faced the outside world once more with all that it offered.

Some N.U.R. And A.S.L.E.F. Men Form Action Group

24-HOUR RAIL STRIKE PLAN AGAINST TRAIN CUTS

A LEICESTER and District Joint Action Committee drawing membership from branches of the National Union of Railwaymen and the Associated Society of Locomotive Enginemen and Firemen, has been formed to fight the Midland Region proposals for the withdrawal of through passenger services on the Great Central line.

Mr. K. G. Issitt, 37, Kingsway, Narborough Road South, Leicester, who has been appointed secretary; points out that the Leicester District Joint Action Committee is to work in collaboration with a similar committee set up at Sheffield.

He adds that a meeting has been held at which approval was given to a resolution calling for a 24-hour protest strike.

This decision has been taken because it is considered that the withdrawals of services are not in the "best interests of British Railways as a whole or of the travelling public."

"It is our intention to oppose them and to urge every possible support for our protest," says Mr. Issitt, who explains that the Midland Region plans mean that Nottingham becomes the new Northern terminal point for travellers to the North on the Marylebone line, and the railway workers themselves feel that the public will prefer to use other routes.

A further meeting of the Leicester Joint Action Committee is planned for early in the New Year when a date is expected to be fixed for the 24-hour protest strike.

MR. K. G. ISSITT

I did my best!

All in favour?

As you can see from the newspaper cutting, I did my best! I did try to get the railways to see sense and reconsider their decision to close the line, but nobody would listen to me! Not only did they decide to withdraw the passenger services on the Great Central line, but their plans included the closure of the direct link to the South West from the Great Central line via Banbury. Just beyond the station at Woodford Halse, about a mile further on, there was a spur that took passengers straight down to Banbury. This connection to the Western line was used by what we called the Bournemouth train. It always seemed to be well patronised. It was a route for Midlanders down towards the south coast.

Footplate men who worked at Leicester Central were given the chance to move en bloc to Leicester Midlands depot, or to anywhere else in the Midland region if there were vacancies. In one way the proposed closures at that time could be understood as there were two lines to the same destination: London. Often these trains would be running less than half full.

It was a time when commuting to London from the Midlands was unusual. If only there had been a crystal ball. Railway travel could have been expanded, road congestion might have been reduced and the use of a safer means of travel could have lessened the number of deaths on the roads. The ingredients were there: business was prospering, bringing more jobs; people generally were enjoying some prosperity; social mobility was increasing and there was optimism in the air in the late 1950s.

It seemed a sad end to what was the last main line to be built but the first main line to close under the Beeching axe of the 1960s.

Goose Fair

Each autumn for 700 years a Goose Fair has been held in Nottingham. Rail companies covered this annual event by laying on special trains over a three-day weekend. Ernie and I were to bring the Goose Fair special back from Nottingham to Leicester on the Sunday. We took a train of empty coaches and brought them back full. Everyone had an excursion ticket.

The police were waiting for us when we got back to Leicester station. I was really glad to see them. First I must explain about the communication cord. The communication cord in a steam train is a chain that runs along the carriage above the door. When pulled it allows air to rush into the train pipe destroying the vacuum – the same action occurs when the driver puts the brake on. The guard then has to close the vent by returning a handle at the end of the coach to the running position. This allows air to be sucked from the train pipe by the driver using the brake mechanism. The vacuum will then be recreated. Up to the day when I was part of the crew that brought the visitors to the Goose Fair back to Leicester, I had never fired a locomotive to anywhere when a communication cord had been pulled. It didn't take long for it to happen on this trip. We pulled away from Nottingham Victoria station at nine o'clock. It was still daylight. The first incident occurred about five minutes into the journey. We had just crossed Trent Bridge and the brake went on. Then it was pulled again as we passed through Ruddington.

It seemed that everyone except my driver, the guard and I was drunk. It took four attempts before we could leave the station precinct. Every time we started someone jumped out of their carriage and ran to the next one. Worse was to come. Each time the cord was pulled I had to get down from the footplate, walk along the track, hoist myself up so that I could open the door and climb into the first carriage. Then I needed to walk down the train to meet the guard who would be coming from the opposite direction, the rear of the train. When the chain was pulled it stayed in that loosened position, so between us we located the carriage with the drooping chain.

'A fine of £5 is payable' was written above the cord. It was no use asking who the culprit was each time – and there were twenty-seven times – because we knew we would not get a serious answer. We simply put the chain back. The guard was a bit apprehensive because we had a trainload of semi-drunken people in high spirits. I knew it was an explosive situation as people in the train were rolling about shouting and singing. They were generally good-natured but I knew that it could easily turn into fighting.

Our greatest worry was that a door would be opened as we were travelling along. Any passenger could do that. There was no means of communicating and no loudspeaker system. I could hear pub songs from one carriage and there was much shouting and rolling about. The customary half-an-hour trip – from Nottingham to Leicester – had become a two-hour one. The train was so late that presumably the police had been alerted and it was assumed that the problem was the usual trouble – drunkenness. It was daylight when we left Nottingham but it was dark when we got back to Leicester.

I had knocked my shins and for days the muscles in my legs were tender.

The doctor

A brass nameplate was attached to the wall at the front of the house. It didn't look as if it had had any attention for a long time. You had to get close to it to see that it advertised the local doctor's surgery with the opening times of his clinic which was held on the next floor, entrance round the back. So I knew that a doctor lived there but I hadn't met him. He was obviously a busy man and one that was not available when I called for my money for cleaning his windows. Three months had gone by, so I determined to ask him for it.

I went in by the back gate, which was my usual habit. I walked up the garden and entered the house through the door that patients were advised to take. As I did so I saw game birds hanging on hooks under the veranda near an outhouse. The outhouse had had an awning put on the top and the outhouse and awning together made what I would call a summerhouse. As I approached the back door I saw three brace of pheasants hanging up in this summerhouse. They were in an advanced state of decay and I could see bluebottles.

A man was sweeping the stairs that went up to the surgery. There was a notice on the wall that read 'Surgery this way' over an arrow that pointed to the top of the stairs. The man was wearing a brown caretaker's jacket and had a yellow duster hanging out of his pocket. He stopped what he was doing when he saw me. I called out, 'I'm looking for the doctor.' He said, 'I am the doctor.' I said, 'Well you owe me three months' money for cleaning your windows.' His forefinger shot up; so did his eyebrows. I had jogged his memory. He said, 'Oh, just a minute,' disappeared for a while, then came back with the cash. There was no problem.

He was the man who told me that pheasant and mild beer go well together and also that I shouldn't drink bitter. 'As much mild as you like,' he said. And that the pheasants in their decaying state would be taken down, plucked and cooked in about another week. He was well known in the neighbourhood and much liked. The only signs of affluence were the pheasants. The whippets that ran round the garden came sheepishly up to me as I went along the untidy path each time I cleaned the windows. I don't think they were house-trained.

The doctor's general manner made me feel at ease. I was pleased to have met him. Without my window cleaning round I would never have done so. I have the erratic railway shifts to thank for that.

Phoebe

'Wait till Phoebe gets you!' chorused the earlier intake of conscripts who were watching us arrive.

We were walking up the drive to the gates of the training camp, a bunch of 18-year-olds just off the train, carrying our cases containing our personal belongings. None of us knew who Phoebe was. We soon found out!

We were a motley crew. We had alighted from the same train, although our homes were scattered. Each of us had chosen to serve our country as a sailor for the eighteen months we were required to do our National Service. I had been called up and had rejected the army and the air force. I had never even seen a naval person in uniform before, not in real life. I did not know that bell-bottoms had to be folded in the way prescribed by the Royal Navy. I did not know that lots of women would touch my collar for luck! A lanyard was a mystery and as for the hat I was to wear, I always thought I looked ridiculous. Tall man with hat!

There he stood – the man sent to fetch us. He wore a shiny peaked cap with a red anchor badge and held a clipboard. He wore a white shirt, a black tie and his sleeves were rolled up. His shoes were highly polished and his trousers well pressed. He shouted, 'All for HMS *Royal Arthur* this way!' and pointed at the van standing outside the station with RN written in large letters on its side. He was waiting for this batch of recruits who now crowded into it; our names were ticked off the list. Then we were driven along the country lanes to the camp. None of us knew what to expect and our reception by the men who shouted from the windows of the huts and from behind the wire that bordered each side of the drive seemed to confirm our worst fears, although we didn't know what they were!

Phoebe cut my hair down to half an inch all over. I could feel the fresh air on my scalp. I looked terrible. I was just 18. This was a young man who wore a DA. I had not met a lady barber before. One young recruit looked as if he hadn't even seen a man barber before. His long tresses waved about in the breeze. I noticed his coat was undone and his hair and the coat were flapping in unison. That was before he met Phoebe.

National Service loomed in front of me. I had temporarily left my railway job and knew I wouldn't return for eighteen months. In the event this turned out to be two years, as someone in Whitehall moved the goalposts. By that time I had joined the ranks of those who met the Royal Navy van with shouts about Phoebe.

Six months after my arrival I climbed aboard my first ship. Eighteen months and three weeks after that I climbed aboard the A3 Pacific locomotive *Sir Frederic Banbury* and resumed my life on the railway.

10

FOG IN THE FIFTIES

My fingers were frozen as I held on to the gantry ladder. I was 30ft from the ground on a very cold and foggy morning. The story I am about to tell illustrates the dangers and difficulties I had on that day. Every footplate man faced similar problems in fog and a good geographical knowledge of the line was necessary and, most importantly, an understanding of the dangers met by other people operating the railway in such weather.

Before smokeless zones were introduced under the Clean Air Acts of 1952 and 1956, fogs – particularly London fogs – were a real hazard for footplate men. These fogs were called smogs and smogs were identified as fogs intensified by smoke. I recall the breakfast train, which became the Master Cutler, which went from Sheffield to London in the mid-1950s. We could hardly see the signal post, never mind the signals. Most people have experienced fog of varying intensity at some time in their lives. But fog in the early fifties was quite different from how it is experienced today. After the war the country was gradually getting into full production and factory chimneys and power stations were pouring out smoke and fumes at an alarming rate. The result was smog. If you stretched your arm out you literally could not see your fingers.

My driver was nearing the end of his career. Freddie had won the Military Medal for bravery when he had rescued two injured soldiers under enemy fire in the First World War. I was glad to be his mate on that day; he knew the line to London as well as anyone and it was very foggy from Leicester Central. Indeed, all the way to London it got progressively worse, particularly from Watford South Junction. On foggy days you really had to know the line.

He had rescued two injured soldiers under
enemy fire in the First World War

You were constantly trying to relate signals to stations, marshalling yards and junctions to where you were. For example, on this day I knew when we were entering Catesby Tunnel that we weren't far from Charwelton water troughs. Even so, we nearly missed them. It was only the different sound we created as we ran over the troughs that alerted me to where we were.

One of the fireman's jobs was to pick up water to fill the tank. He would lower a scoop, mounted below the tender, by turning the scoop handle which was situated on the tender opposite the tender brake. The scoop lowered into a trough full of water that sat between the rails on the track. Due to the length of the troughs, 500–600 yards, a fireman had to be ready to drop the scoop as soon as he came to them. As the train would be travelling at 50 or 60mph, it was easy to miss the troughs. In good, clear weather it was relatively easy to pick up water successfully – there were signs indicating that troughs were ahead. In winter, ice brought its own problems, of course. When the fireman had fog to deal with, the importance of knowing the position of the troughs became vital. It was the sound that the movement of the train made as it travelled over the troughs that was the guide and that, added to the crew's knowledge of the track, meant that the tank would be filled. As he did this the fireman had to watch the water gauge on the tender carefully, otherwise when the tank was full, water would shoot out of the top of the tender. Muscle was required to withdraw the scoop blade against the force of the water in the trough.

We had an A3 Pacific on this foggy day. The capacity of the tank was 5,300 gallons. This would not be sufficient to take us all the way to London with a ten-coach train without taking on more water. We would have had to stop at Aylesbury if we had missed the troughs at Charwelton. Fortunately, we didn't. The fog was dense and I had to rely on my sense of hearing more than I had ever done before.

If you own a car and you think you know the road you can still be disorientated in heavy fog. You can say that at least we were on rails, but the fog creates an eerie effect that plays havoc with your senses. Your sight is severely curtailed so other senses are heightened, like smell, touch, hearing and even taste. For instance, I always knew we were near Lutterworth in Leicestershire by the smell of the ironworks at the foundry. I could even taste the acrid fumes. When you went over a viaduct there was a certain distinctive sound that gave an indication of where you were.

Platelayers had to be extra careful when performing their duties on the track because fog deadens sound. Trains could be on you before your ears detected their approach. A platelayer had a length of track to maintain, requiring daily inspection of the rails; wooden wedges were used to keep the rail tightly in its mounting. The mounting was on the sleeper and the wedge was pushed between the rail and the mounting. The vibration from the trains meant these wedges tended to get loose. There was a need for constant maintenance of the track. On one occasion a platelayer was killed in a fog at Whetstone in Leicestershire. I was on shed duties at the time. The engine was brought back to Leicester loco for an inspection in which I was involved. Platelaying in the fifties was a very labour-intensive job. Wooden wedges are no longer used and a different system of holding the rail in place has since been designed.

It certainly comes home to you how dangerous your place of work can be when people are killed or seriously injured when weather conditions change dramatically. People working along the tracks of high-speed trains needed to be constantly vigilant. The platelayer in his daily duties had no warnings to tell him that a train was approaching from either direction, only his eyesight and hearing. When that was curtailed, as on the occasion I have described, when two senses are severely affected and you have the unenviable job of inspecting the external and inside motions of the engine that killed the unfortunate platelayer, it can be seen how hazardous the job can be.

Missing a distant signal puts you into no-man's-land, so to speak. You don't know whether the signal is still to come, or whether you've passed it, so you have to drop your speed down to a crawl until you come to a stop signal – and you could easily slip by that too if you were not extra careful. Junctions were extremely dangerous places if you missed a signal, as you can imagine, and we had no bells or anything to tell us that we had passed the signals. Often the signalman would shout to us to let us know that the line was clear to the next section and sometimes it was signal box to signal box – that's if the box was alongside the line. But at junctions the box was set back from several sets of line so it wasn't possible to shout to the signalman. The only way to speak to him was to cross the lines. This was hazardous as you did not know who had the right of way because you couldn't see the signals – even the electric signals were down to the size of golf balls when you came upon them.

On this occasion we were both looking out for signals. We had already had a distant signal against us. I was over on my driver's side and we were both hanging well outside the cab, straining our eyes in case we should slip by a signal and into the path of a train that could be coming across us. This was a busy junction. In spite of our care, we had passed the signal gantry; passing it was the very thing we were trying to avoid. I couldn't tell by how far but we

I inched my way
along the catwalk

guessed half an engine length. We still didn't know whether the signal was off or on, so there was urgency in our situation.

That we had a trainload of passengers to deliver safely was our prime concern. But to get them to their destination on time was out of the question.

The question could be asked: 'How did you know which junction you were at?' The answer is that we were unsure.

I climbed down from the engine and ran back as quickly as I could. I couldn't rush because I couldn't see. I was stumbling over the slippery sleepers with my arms outstretched trying to feel for the signal post. I reached the ladder, which was ice cold. I ascended it gingerly, finally reaching the catwalk at the top of the ladder, which was about 30ft above the ground. My thoughts went to the lamp lads whose job it was to climb up the signal posts to clean and replenish the lamps with paraffin every day. Oil lamps lit the majority of signals in those days. I hadn't realised how dangerous a lamp lad's job was until I was faced with having to climb the signal ladder myself, in icy conditions and in thick fog. I had never done this before. Having an eye on my own safety I inched my way along the catwalk. I had to let go of the handrail to reach up to the signal boards so I had to maintain my balance as I stepped across the narrow catwalk. I grabbed the signal post to steady myself. The fog had enveloped me.

The whole scene was quite dramatic. We had an express train with several hundred passengers. It all seemed to depend on me. None of the passengers knew anything about it; neither did the guard who was ten carriages away. The only person who knew what was happening was my driver, Freddie, and since the engine was blowing off steam, he would not have heard me shout and could not see me. He, too, was relying on me.

It was only when I had climbed the signal post ladder and reached the gantry on which the signals were mounted that I found out we were at Neasden South Junction. I knew the signal arrangement.

There were four sets of signals on the gantry: two loop lines with distant signals; one main line, also with a distant signal; and one post with two siding signals on it. I needed the third post that held the signals for the main line. I edged along the catwalk counting the posts as I went. I got to the third post. I reached up and felt the signal boards. They were in the upper quadrant position, which meant that we could proceed on our journey. Had the signals been in the horizontal position we would have been in very serious trouble because we had passed the signals that govern the path of the trains that cut across our main line.

My fingers were numb. When I was up there, 30ft above the ground, my balance seemed to be affected, as I couldn't relate to anything. I was actually above the coaches, but I could not see them. My fingers were so cold and I was very much aware that my grip on the ladder had to be firm as I descended.

I reached the ground and staggered back to the warmth of the footplate. I told Freddie that the signals were off and we had right of way. We were both so relieved.

Freddie was anxious about my welfare. When we finally got to London – about 5 miles away – I was able to explain to him what I had done. 'Well, I certainly couldn't have got up there,' he said. I felt that to be a big compliment.

11

FROM CHRIS'S STUDIO

12

BACKSTAGE

The black pad

An elephant handler in Sri Lanka, a mahout, spends most of his life with elephants, learning to understand them and not to be fazed by their size and power. During the time that a footplate man is learning his job he gets used to handling engines weighing many tons and he too is not fazed by their size and power. The foreman put this in his own words one night when he said quite mildly, 'Blimey! Another few yards and it would have been in the cut!'

There was a bright moon and the skies were clear. I had pedalled the 3 miles from home for my early morning shift. I freewheeled down the black pad for 200–300 yards. The black pad got its name because it was made up of ashes and coal dust. It wound its way from the end of the pavement down by the side of the allotments to the footpath at the edge of the canal. It then went into the loco sheds that were sited close to the canal. The canal was a source of water for the water columns that provided the water for the engine tenders. As the path turned sharp left, I was aware that I was facing the moon. I was then parallel with the canal. The moonlight had thrown the loco sheds into silhouette. They, too, were in front of me. I could see the moonlight reflecting on the water and the lock gates were only a few yards away. The surface of the water was silvery and shimmering.

As I got nearer to the sheds I could see that there was something wrong. The end of the shed didn't look right. I stared. I got off my bike and went really close to the wall to have a proper look. I could see the smokebox of an engine sticking through the end of the shed wall. What's more, there was a

I could see the smokebox of an engine
sticking through the end of the shed wall

*The foreman rubbed his eyes, came out
of his doze and stared at me*

swirl of smoke coming out of the engine chimney. I could see the front bogey
wheels. Once I was sure that what I was seeing was real I remounted my bike
and pedalled to the bike sheds. My immediate thought was that surely they all
knew. They would have heard the bricks falling down as the engine pushed its
way through the wall. So I put my bike in the bike shed, walked to the stores,
booked on and then went to the foreman's office.

'Does anyone know about the engine with its smokebox sticking out of
the shed end on number 3 bay?' I said, quietly.

The foreman rubbed his eyes, came out of his doze and stared at me. He
stood up. I realised then that nobody knew.

'Eh? Yer what?'

I repeated myself, a little louder this time.

'There's an engine with its smokebox sticking out the end of the shed!'

Without another word the foreman strode out of the office and ran down
the shed to see for himself. The foreman's office and the end of Bay 3 were a
long way from each other. I wandered into the mess room. I asked the lads in
there who were playing cards what I had just asked the foreman. 'He knows
then, does he?' one asked, jerking his head towards the foreman's office with a
grin. I nodded. No one got up; they simply waited for the foreman to return.
Sure enough the mess room door was flung open. 'Blimey! Another few yards
and it would have been in the cut.'

The card game continued. No one moved. The fact that an engine weighing over 100 tons had sailed down the shed on its own, ploughed through the wall and finished up about 30ft from the canal didn't seem to bother anyone. It failed to raise hardly an eyebrow above the card game.

Then it was:

'Only needed a little more steam in the steam chest and that would've done it.'

And then:

'Good job you noticed it.'

The engine had been lit up to raise steam in preparation for its journey later on in the day. It had been left in forward gear. The regulator was not shut properly, the handbrake was off and the cylinder taps were shut. When steam started to generate in the boiler, 50 psi was all it needed to set the engine in motion, so off it went, right down number 3 bay and through the shed end. There were no buffers at the end of each bay because they were not considered to be necessary. This was a working area for the fitters, where engines were repaired and were not in steam. There was a pit under each bay that ran the full length of the shed. If the fitters wanted to move an engine that was out of steam they would use pinch bars.

On this night there were no engines on number 3 bay for repair so the errant engine had a clear run, straight through the brick wall. This was the talk of the mess room for days and nobody ever knew who left the engine in forward gear with the taps shut because no one ever owned up!

The mess room

In the mess room there was a large open fire. It was always roaring away and this was particularly welcome in the winter. It was a place where train crews congregated after they had booked on duty, before they left the loco sheds with their engine en route to the station, or when they had finished their shift and were ready to go home. Sometimes it was full of footplate staff. Some of them were playing cards – solo and three-card brag were the favourite games. There were two tables. One accommodated the two-card schools and the other was marked out for shove ha'penny.

The larger of the two tables was placed immediately in front of the fire. Sometimes there would be as many onlookers as players; some stood and some found themselves a seat. Even if they were not playing cards there would be an avid interest in the game – a few preferring to watch the tactics

In the mess room there was a large open fire

of the players. Men were coming and going all the time. There was a general hubbub. There were chats about all sorts of things, from union business to current affairs, to recent trips, the weather (which was an important topic for railwaymen), to the state of the engines themselves.

'Have you been on 61028 lately? It's a terrible ride. It's loose between the engine and the tender. Coal's coming down all the time. I couldn't keep pace with the coal coming down on the footplate.'

When we learned that the line was to be closed there was even more chat. Railwaymen frequented pubs and clubs and went to union meetings, all of which were subjects of conversation in the mess room.

Shove ha'penny was not quite as popular. It didn't draw such a busy crowd. The table was situated further away from the fire, and although the

Shove ha'penny was not quite as popular.
It didn't draw such a busy crowd

There were two tables. One accommodated the two-card schools

players gambled and were keen, it was seen as just another game to play. There were some very sharp card players, however, and they attracted a great deal of interest.

One enterprising loco man had a large suitcase in which he carried cigarettes, sweets, chocolates and Turkey red handkerchiefs. He brought this into the mess room and was always ready to sell to anyone willing to buy. He even had a tab so that men could pay him at the end of the week.

The mess room was also a place for eating, mashing tea, having a fag and a moan or two. But generally there was a friendly, welcoming atmosphere borne out of the camaraderie of the loco men, all with recent incidents to talk about.

Disaster struck! As soon as I put the shovel
back into the firebox - 'swoosh' - the whole
kaboodle was pulled off the shovel

The blower

My initiation into the world of cooking my breakfast on the shovel, which many think is part of the life of a footplate man – a 'bonus' if you like – happened like this.

I did as I had been told. I stood on the footplate and got the shovel really hot – red hot in fact – by sticking the blade of the shovel into the firebox and then quenching it under the water tap on the tender. Then I gave it a good wipe with a clean rag ready for the food I had brought with me, which was in my bag in the locker on the footplate. I then had to warm the shovel up again so I put it back into the firebox. When it was hot I withdrew it and placed my lump of lard in the centre. I collected the other ingredients (one egg, two slices of bacon, two large slices of bread and two tomatoes) and arranged them carefully in the spitting fat on the shovel.

There are two forms of draught employed in locomotives. One is natural draught and the other is induced draught. A valve mounted on the driver's side of the faceplate operates the blower jet, or the 'blower', which is the way that footplate men generally refer to it. When it is opened it creates an induced draught obtained by turning a jet of steam up the chimney, emptying the smokebox of air. The vacuum then created induces air through the fire bar interspaces and the fire hole door if it is open, filling the void. The blower jet or cone of steam is mounted on the blast pipe situated in the smokebox.

The blower is vital for the safety of footplate men. It is imperative that the blower is working when the regulator is shut. When the engine is coming to a stop in a station the driver must put the blower on before he shuts the regulator. Otherwise a serious blowback is inevitable. Also, he must make sure that it is open before entering tunnels when moving downhill because an induced draught is necessary.

Disaster struck! As soon as I put the shovel back into the firebox – 'swoosh' – the whole egg and bacon kaboodle was pulled off the shovel. My breakfast disappeared into the flames. I had turned the blower on too much and the draught sucked my breakfast away. I had not realised the valve needed to be cracked just a tiny bit.

One thing I learnt, though – it's not possible to cook a breakfast and fire a train at the same time!

Shunting in the marshalling yards, on the other hand, meant that there would be regular breaks and waiting times in a siding. These were the best times to fry up!

13

ANOTHER RIGHT MESS

In the normal way you had to dampen down the footplate area with what we called the degger pipe to keep the dust down while the engine was moving. It was a constant job because inevitably, as you fired the engine coal dust would find its way into all the nooks and crevices on the footplate. It was important to keep on top of it. But this story shows that when things start to go wrong, the normal procedures have to wait their turn.

We left Leicester one early July evening so most of the journey to Sheffield was in daylight. But as we gradually approached Sheffield it was becoming dusk and there was a gradual change in the landscape. The freshness of the green fields in Leicestershire was replaced by meadows coated with the pollution of the industrial city. Sheffield seemed to have a special smell associated with the steel mills and ironworks, and the bricks of many buildings were streaked with black.

A Leicester crew had brought the London to Sheffield semi-fast passenger train as far as Leicester. It was a Leicester changeover. The engine had been uncoupled and we had backed up on to the train with a Sheffield-based engine. The reason for this unusual situation was that a Leicester engine had failed at Sheffield the day before so Sheffield had provided an engine to take its place. We were returning this loaned engine and therefore were scheduled to bring the Leicester engine back to Leicester depot on the Night Mail in the early hours of the following morning.

There were three stops on our route. The first was Loughborough, the second Nottingham Victoria and the third Chesterfield. At Loughborough our line crossed the Midland Railway. Trains from the Midland Railway

We left Leicester one early July evening

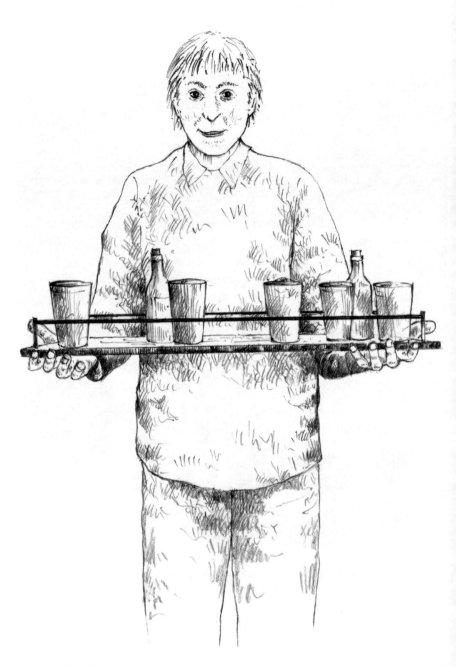

From where apprentice boys would come with
trays specially made to carry beer

also stopped at Loughborough but they took a different route. They went on to Derby whilst we went on to Nottingham Victoria. We passed through Ruddington and over the River Trent.

We entered the tunnel immediately at the south end of Nottingham Victoria station and drew into the station itself. There were high walls around the station, which was far lower than the street, and in order to get to street level you had to climb a series of steps. There were facilities for an engine to be turned round, and an ash pit and water columns for the use of the crews of trains that terminated here.

The next stop was Chesterfield, a picturesque market town in the Peak District. Its focal point is the twisted spire of the parish church of St Mary's and All Saints that passengers could see as the train dropped down into the station. One legend has it that the twisted spire was the work of the devil. A rather more likely reason is that the unseasoned wood used in its construction resulted in the warping of the timber. This parish church, built in the fourteenth century with a spire 70m high and clad with lead, leans over 3m from the centre.

We passed a mink farm on our right after we left Chesterfield. It was laid out in a series of enclosures for the animals to run up and down – rather like chicken runs – which we could see clearly as we passed. The mink were being bred for their pelts.

It was almost dark as we ran down into Sheffield station in the heart of the city itself. The industrial nature of the town was emphasised by the dusk. Steel mills were in full production and the fumes and smoke from the chimneys hung over the city. The Clean Air Acts of 1952 and 1956 had not yet come fully into force and the pollution from the steel factories had blackened the walls of the buildings. The steelworks were very close to the station precincts. There were very high walls in and around one side of the station and the steel mills were directly at the back of those walls. There appeared to be no houses anywhere near, but let into the high walls there was a pub. The pub was open. If we visited it in the evening there was little activity, but in the daytime – at lunchtime – the pub was alive with custom from the steelworks, from where apprentice boys would come with trays specially made to carry beer, which they took back to the works where temperatures were so high that the men working there needed lots of liquid.

We ran into Sheffield Victoria on time and were met by Sheffield men ('grinders' – a nickname used to describe Sheffield train crews because of their association with the steel industry) who relieved us and took their engine to the loco. When one crew replaced another on the footplate it was

The coal hammer was a vital part of the kit on the footplate, alongside the shovel

known as 'relieving'. We had two hours before we were due to leave Sheffield to return to Leicester to bring the mail train. This train had started in Manchester and we were to take it forward from Sheffield back to Leicester. Since we were waiting for our Leicester engine from Sheffield loco and were relieved by the grinders, we did not have to go onto the turntable in the station precincts, get water and clean the fire. We killed time on the station platform. The Manchester train duly came and members of the station staff were busy loading and unloading mail. We were still waiting for our engine. It finally appeared barely fifteen minutes before we were due to leave.

As soon as I got on to the footplate I busied myself raising steam ready for the journey. We had eleven coaches to pull. I could have done with another ten minutes or so to get a full head of steam because I knew there was an incline fairly soon after leaving Sheffield station. The engine backed up to the train with 150 psi of steam and I needed 220 psi. I was left with virtually no time to get the engine prepared properly for its task. The boiler was only half full. I confess I was agitated. But the whistle blew and the guard waved his flag and off we went. Albert and I both realised that this was not a perfect situation.

All engines shedded at Sheffield were fuelled with hopper-fed coal, unlike those at Leicester, where all the coal on the tender was hand-shovelled and stacked on the tender. Large lumps were broken up and stacked so that the coal fell towards you as you fired the engine. As Leicester was a fast train depot, the coal was already broken into sizeable pieces to enable the fireman to fire the engine without spending time cracking large lumps. It was cracked and stacked for him. But Sheffield had hopper-fed coal. A wagon full of coal was hauled up the side of the hopper mechanically and the entire contents of the wagon were tipped into the hopper. The total weight was often 30 tons or more. Large lumps, coal dust and small coal were all mixed up. Consequently, the fireman had to crack these large lumps as they fell forward into the well of the tender before he could fire the engine properly. The demand for fuel in the firebox at the Leicester loco, where the engines needed constant firing when hauling fast trains, was different from the needs at Sheffield. A Sheffield fireman did not have the advantage of ready-stacked coal. In both cases the coal was fired through a trap on the fire door when the engine was running along and that controlled the airflow into the firebox and assisted combustion.

The coal hammer was a vital part of the kit on the footplate, alongside the shovel, the detonators and the gauge lamp. The gauge lamp was used at night to illuminate the gauge glass, which in turn showed the level of the water in the boiler. About a mile out of Sheffield a very large lump dropped into the well of the tender. It was too big to go into the firebox, even with the big fire door open. I reached for the coal hammer. No coal hammer! There was an empty space where the hammer should have been. I looked everywhere. No sign. Panic. I managed to lever the huge lump of coal on to the footplate with the shovel in the hope that I could get at smaller coal to continue firing. I pushed the lump to one side of the footplate but unfortunately yet more large lumps fell into the well.

I shouted to my driver, 'Is the coal hammer in your corner?' and he looked briefly but couldn't see it. I knew I had to get this coal broken and looked round for something I could use to break it with. The only choice I had was to use the pivotal brake handle on the tender. This was mounted on the

I lifted the lump bodily and dropped it on to the handle several times

right-hand side of the tender. A steel peg protruded from it vertically for about 6in.

This peg was the handle and was used to apply the tender brake by rotating the handle clockwise. I lifted the huge lump bodily and dropped it on to the handle several times. We were still moving, increasing speed and the engine and tender were rocking from side to side as usual. This added to the problem. The coal eventually broke up into smaller pieces which I threw into the firebox with my bare hands because the lumps were not small enough to fire through the trap. I had no gloves; they were not obligatory and I found they made me sweat. Albert could see what was happening but had to keep his eyes on the track and could not help me. As I was unable to fire the engine correctly I was losing ground in maintaining steam. Every time I tried to fire it yet another huge lump came down.

Albert shortened the valve travel to the point that would minimise the demand for steam and water. This way he was still able to keep going, but as we were gradually climbing uphill we were travelling slower and slower. The danger was that if we dropped down too much in steam pressure the brake on the entire train would stop the train. A minimum of 100 psi was needed; any less than that would mean too little power to maintain the vacuum in the brake pipe throughout the train. My method of cracking coal by smacking the lump down on the tender handle brake seemed to work but coal and coal dust flew everywhere. The footplate was eventually covered in a thick layer of coal and the coal dust appeared to be dancing with the movement of the engine.

I couldn't do anything about the haze that was enveloping the footplate and I had no time to clear up the coal that was everywhere. Albert, watching the steam pressure falling back, had to adjust the demand on the engine in order to conserve the steam and water in the boiler. He used his skill as a driver and his knowledge of the gradients; he knew full well that if we could get by Tibshelf and through Annesley then the run down into Nottingham would mean minimal demands on the steam and water in the boiler. We only just made it to the top of the gradient; the speed was down to a crawl. We coasted down into Annesley. Albert was able to shut the regulator. The demand for steam was not required. We coasted through Annesley and all the way downhill to Nottingham Victoria. I was able to bring the engine back up to full pressure and to fill the boiler. My thoughts on the way down were that at least I had got the engine back to a full head of steam, but I wondered if there would be a station pilot at Nottingham who would lend me his coal hammer. There were still plenty of lumps to crack.

Once in Nottingham Victoria I jumped off the engine and looked for the station pilot. Fortunately I could see him. He was at the other end of the station, in a siding. I ran the full length of the platform. 'Could I have your coal hammer, mate? I've had to manage all the way from Sheffield without one!' I ran back to the engine with the coal hammer in my hand and two minutes later we were off. Now I had time to clear up the footplate a little so that it was back to normal when we arrived at Leicester.

The rest of the journey was comparatively easy. I was able to crack the lumps and keep a full head of steam. We left the train at Leicester Central

*My overalls had to be scrubbed
with a scrubbing brush*

We looked like a pair of chimney sweeps

station as a fresh engine was ready to take it forward to London. We climbed off the footplate and looked at each other in our sorry states. We were absolutely black from head to foot. Just little rings of white remained around our eyes where we had been squinting to look for signals. The dust had settled on our faces like a mask where we had been perspiring. We looked like a pair of chimney sweeps. Albert had been attacked by coal dust but I had the additional discomfort of splinters of coal all over my face as a result of banging the lumps. They were finding their way down my neck, into my ears, up my legs and the dust was in my overalls and clothing. And my fingers were raw. 'Can I have a sweet every time I come?' I said to the nurse at the Eye Clinic after she had picked splinters of coal and ash out of my eyes yet again. My overalls had to be scrubbed with a scrubbing brush after I laid them out on the kitchen table the next day.

That I did not check that a coal hammer was on the footplate became a lesson I never forgot. I always made sure that before I ever left a depot or a station the coal hammer was on board!

14

ATTEMPTED MURDER?

I am very aware that the design of railway locomotives has changed since the end of the steam era. Everything is designed for maximum efficiency. As there is now no need for a fireman, one person drives the locomotive. In the tale I am about to tell, the reader will understand that I was very grateful to be one of two people on the footplate that day.

The question about whether it is better to have one or two persons on the footplate can be looked at in opposing ways. Today's driver looks through a windscreen with a full view of the track. His reactions have to be extremely sharp. Today's trains are, on the whole, travelling much faster than in the days of steam so the margins for error are narrower. They are regularly achieving over 100mph. Trains sometimes leave stations within five minutes of each other. The timings between trains are very close and punctuality is foremost in the train schedule. Perhaps today's travelling public would be more assured about safety if there were two people at the controls rather than one – like a co-pilot in an aircraft. The driver of the steam train had the full length of the boiler restricting his wider view. When the steam engine travelled round curves the driver had to rely on his fireman to check the signals. In effect, this became a double security check. Further, if there was a mishap – the footplate was a working area and there was always the possibility of a tumble or a slip, especially when running at high speed – there was someone there to help you, as I was able to help Cyril on this occasion.

Reassurance, too, was always valuable, however much experience each man had. Two pairs of eyes are better than one, it is said. Several incidents in the recent past have convinced me that had two people been on the locomotives at the time, then those incidents could have been avoided. What has been lost in double-checking, however, has been made up for in the telecommunication system and more sophisticated signalling. And, of course, people are more in contact with the driver, who is more accessible than he ever was on steam locomotives. Safety systems are at the disposal of the driver – dead man's handle, alarm bells and all the benefits of telecommunication for instance – but my view is that two people are better than one. This is what happened one day in the mid-1950s.

Cyril and I booked on duty at lunchtime one winter day to work the South Yorkshireman to London and back. We had an A3 Pacific but I can't recall its name. We left the loco sheds en route to the station and the South Yorkshireman duly arrived. After the usual changeover we were on our way.

We had an uneventful journey to London. We arrived on time and in the late afternoon started our return journey. It was just becoming dusk.

Immediately after we left the station precincts we entered the tunnels and climbed, emerging alongside the Metropolitan line on the way to Neasden and beyond. The track at this point was quite high above the ground and there was a series of high-rise flats alongside. Well, as the tunnels were full of smoke it was good to get past them and back into the fresh air. Our speed increased as we sped along towards Neasden South Junction.

I was busy firing when suddenly Cyril shouted, 'Something's hit me! I've been hit!' I stopped, turned and saw that Cyril was holding his head in both hands.

It was dark by this time and difficult to see anything properly. The only light came from the glare of the firebox. Our speed was 50 to 60mph and the footplate was rocking from side to side, as it normally did. I helped Cyril out of his seat, put my arm around him to steady him as he was staggering, and guided him across the footplate towards my seat, leaving the controls to themselves. I now could see him a little better as the glare of the fire provided me with the best light I could get. There was blood trickling down his face from his eye. Leaving him momentarily, I grabbed the controls. I had to take his place. 'Hang on, Cyril. I'll stop at Neasden South and tell them what's happened.' I needed to know, very quickly and precisely, where we were, as we would be reaching Neasden South Junction any minute. I knew that Cyril must have taken his eyes off the track after he was hit.

It took me a few seconds to get my bearings. Fortunately, all signals were at green so I knew we hadn't missed any and as those signals were controlling the junction at Neasden South I knew where we were. I decided to stop the train at the signal box. Realising that I had brought the train to a standstill across a junction I clambered down the steps on the driver's side and ran. The

There was blood trickling down his face from his eye

signal box was set back from several sets of lines and the signalman saw me running towards him. As I ran I was aware that I had left Cyril on his own. The signalman was standing at the window, yelling, 'What the hell are you doing? You're blocking all main lines!' I breathlessly explained what had happened. 'Well, you can't stop here,' he said. 'I'm just telling you the situation,' I said. He said, 'Can you get to Aylesbury? I can wire you on and get relief and medical help there.' I could see that there wasn't much choice. Aylesbury, I realised, was the only place where I could get attention and relief for Cyril. I ran back to Cyril and moved him back into his seat, as he had recovered a little by then, but he was still in great pain and discomfort. I asked him whether he could hold on until we got to Aylesbury. He said, 'There's nothing else for it, we'll have to go.' I checked frequently to see how he was and between us we managed to get to Aylesbury.

Alas, when we reached Aylesbury there was no relief driver and no chance of getting one, as the station staff explained to me. A relief driver would have had to come either from Neasden or from Woodford Halse, as Aylesbury is midway between the two. So there we were, with a trainload of passengers, the station staff having done their job, their faces showing anxiety, particularly as this was the South Yorkshireman, a prestigious train. They were looking to us to make a decision. We had no one to advise us. We had to make the decision for ourselves. We looked at each other. Cyril could receive medical help at Aylesbury but to organise and get a relief driver from either Neasden or Woodford Halse would take at least two hours. The South Yorkshireman would be left standing in the platform at Aylesbury for that length of time, probably for longer. I said, 'What do you think, mate? Can you hold on?' and Cyril, like the man he was, said, 'We'll have a go.'

On reflection, maybe it wasn't the wisest thing to do. I was anxious. I had to keep looking over at Cyril to make sure he had not collapsed as he was very shaken up. I knew his sight would be blurred at the least. I was also aware that the responsibility of the train was now, in effect, mine.

I have always considered footplate work to be a two-man job. Cyril did his job and I did mine. We worked as a team. Suddenly, this partnership altered as Cyril was unable to do his part. Not only was half the team inactive but there was an injury that needed attention. Fortunately, the engine had a good head of steam and the water level was adequate so I could leave my duties and assist Cyril. I knew that the train could proceed as usual for some distance without my attention so I took temporary charge of the footplate. I knew exactly where we were. I was a senior fireman and I knew the route well, so I did not think there was any danger to the passengers or us. I was not fazed and did not panic. Danger could have come from the attentions of a less experienced fireman.

Thankfully, when we arrived at Woodford Halse a driver was waiting. Cyril went straight to hospital. He never drove again. He finished his time on the railway doing odd jobs around the loco sheds. Although he retained his driver's pay, it was the end of his career as a fast train driver.

Cyril lost the sight in that eye. Maybe prompt attention would have saved it. We will never know. Personally, I regarded him as a man on top of his job and it was a pleasure to work with him. I had complete confidence in his abilities in a job where we had to rely on each other so much.

I understood later that there had been reports of rifle shots breaking carriage windows in the area. It seemed to me that the would-be assassin had become bolder. He had been shooting at the trains, breaking windows without too much aim, and thought, 'let's see if we can put the driver or fireman away'. He took careful aim at the driver, whose position at the controls would be known, with head, shoulders and elbow protruding from the cab. A3 Pacifics had a deflector as protection on the cab window, but the angle from which the shot was fired as we moved along meant that Cyril's head was exposed as we came more into the line of fire. I suspect that a high-powered air rifle was used. No one was ever caught. If he had been, what would have been the charge? Attempted murder?

Questions and answers about 'Attempted Murder?'

I am aware that the reader may be left high and dry after reading this story. There are questions to ask. There were no clear rules about what to do in such circumstances and the reader may query my decisions. So, in answer to any anticipated questions and to answer my own, I have written a set of Questions and Answers. Answer a) is what I would have given had I been asked at the time, and answer b) is how I would answer questions about the incident if I was asked now.

1. Was the incident reported to the police?
a) Not the police, no. I reported it to the signalman. The signalman knew that I had stopped the train and why I had done so.
b) As soon as I was clear of my duties I would have reported the matter to the running foreman and would expect a visit from the railway police at any time.

'Let's see if we can put the driver or fireman away'

2. But did you have to tell the police?

a) No. Not me. The signalman had explained to the signalman at Aylesbury what had happened. He knew we needed help and that we needed to get to Aylesbury to get that help. In answer to the question, the police never contacted me. But Cyril may have been contacted.

b) I would expect to make a full report.

3. Did you tell anyone?

a) Yes, when I eventually got back to the Leicester locomotive sheds I explained to the running foreman in the office what had happened, as well, of course, as the signalman at Neasden South. The foreman knew about it but I gave him the details.

b) Again, I would expect to make out a full report. Also, I would think that it would be suggested that I attend a meeting about the incident and that I get checked over by a nurse or doctor. It would be important, too, to have a few days' sick leave. The union representative did not approach me. Perhaps he didn't need to, if all he was dealing with was Cyril's compensation and safeguarding his interests. He knew about it because he was a railway employee himself. I did not approach him as I thought it was all being dealt with.

4. You have entitled this story 'Attempted Murder?' So were you questioned by the police? Did you expect to be?

a) I thought I would be but I heard nothing more about it.

b) I would have thought that this was a case of attempted murder so I did expect to be questioned by the police, partly for them to analyse what happened and partly to help them catch the person who fired the gun. It is only recently that I have realised that the angle at which Cyril was struck is the clue to the fact that someone deliberately took aim. I consider that I myself was partly to blame, too. I should have insisted that someone listened to me properly instead of leaving it all to those I thought would have taken the whole subject further.

5. Did the railway acknowledge what you did on that day?

a) No.

b) No, they certainly did not. And I think they should have done.

6. But in the light of the fact that you had a trainload of passengers, surely you would have heard from the Head Office?

a) But I didn't.

b) I expected a full inquiry to take place in the near future, especially as I, as fireman, was in charge of a train full of passengers.

7. You say in the story that you perhaps should have made a different decision. What would that have been?

a) I could have said no, my driver has been seriously injured and I need help so I am not moving this train.

b) I would not have gone to Aylesbury. I would possibly have stopped at Harrow-on-the-Hill. I would have made sure that Cyril went to hospital and the whole train would have had to wait in that station until a relief driver arrived. I could have cleared the junction – about which the signalman was so anxious – and stopped at the next station.

8. Could you have done that?

a) Yes, I had the power. It was up to me. Even if Cyril had argued with me and said 'carry on' I could have said, 'no, you are going to hospital.'

b) The answer would be the same.

9. So why didn't you?

a) There were no buildings or people. The signalman was shouting to me to move. The only communication was through him. It was a dramatic situation and I thought we could get help at Aylesbury. The signalman assured me that a relief driver and medical help would be available there. If I had known that there would be no relief driver and no medical help there this would have affected my decision. Aware that either way there would be a delay of at least a couple of hours I decided, with Cyril's agreement, that to move on was the best thing to do, not to just clear the junction and stop. We needed to be where there was help. If we simply cleared the junction help was not accessible. I would still have made the same decision, to get Cyril closer to help.

b) I would answer this question in exactly the same way.

10. In the light of what happened do you feel that you did everything you could to help Cyril?

a) Yes, but sometimes I wonder. I was very bothered about Cyril's welfare.

b) What was running through my head was this: the junction could not function whilst we occupied it. This meant that other trains could not pass across the junction until we were out of the way. Also, we were at a great distance from any help; it was dark; I had an engine there blowing off steam needing my attention. We had a trainload of passengers who were our responsibility, and the decision I made with Cyril's agreement was that we went forward to Aylesbury. We did not, of course, know how serious the injury was – we simply could not see properly because it was dark and the only light was from the glare from the firebox. The ideal situation would have been if a relief driver and an ambulance man had come to the train and taken Cyril to hospital. But we did not even have a first-aid box. The guard walked through the carriages to the front of the train to find out what was happening. His head was out of the first carriage window and I shouted, 'Cyril's been hit in the eye, mate. We are heading for Aylesbury.' And that is what we did.

11. Were you shaken up?

a) Yes, because I was worried about Cyril and because I had taken on full responsibility for the decisions that were made.

b) Yes. Very shaken. The whole affair shook me up. My senses were sharpened at the time. When it happened I had no time to think about myself. I thought about Cyril, the train and the passengers. If such a thing happened now I certainly would expect to have a few days' leave and to have some advice from a doctor. I am afraid that I did what many working men did – got on with it! I simply went to work the next day.

15

EGGS AND BLUELEGS

This picture of a leaflet about dried eggs issued by the Ministry of
Food shows one of the ways in which we dealt with the shortage of
eggs during the war years. Dried egg was sent to Britain as a result of the
Lend-Lease Bill of 1941 from America. This finished in 1946, three days after
the victory over Japan. From then until 1954, when all rationing ceased –
roughly the date of this story – the egg industry was not up and running.
The frugal years of the war still lived with us and it was still quite something
to acquire a dozen eggs in the way I will describe. This was a time, of course,
before broiler chickens, battery hens and factory farming. Harold, my driver,
and I were city people and to get eggs in the way we did caused us to feel
that somehow we had cheated the system. However, there was an added
element of adventure, too. Harold rubbed his hands together and said, 'Two
eggs for breakfast, eh, mate?'

We used to work a local passenger train, stopping at all stations between
Leicester Great Northern station and Grantham, and we knew a local farmer
on this route. The irony was that we never actually saw him; we understood
that he was blind but because we hadn't seen him we didn't know whether he
was or not. But we felt we knew him because when we wanted some eggs and
left our bucket with five shillings in it for a dozen, they were always there. We
would drop our speed down to a crawl and I would stand on the bottom step
of the engine and drop the bucket off beside the crossing gate, giving a 'pop
pop' on the whistle to let him know that the bucket was there with the money
in it. Then we would carry on to Grantham. After we had arrived at Grantham
we turned the engine on the turntable, filled the tank and made our way to

"DRIED EGGS
are <u>my</u> eggs—
my <u>whole</u> eggs
and
nothing but my eggs"

Dried eggs are the complete hen's eggs, both the white and the yolk, dried to a powder. Nothing is added. Nothing but moisture and the shell taken away, leaving the eggs themselves as wholesome, as digestible and as full of nourishment and health-protecting value as if you had just taken the eggs new laid from the nest. So put the eggs back into your breakfast menus. And what about a big, creamy omelette for supper? You can have it savoury; or sweet, now that you get extra jam.

DRIED EGGS build you up!

In war-time, the most difficult foods for us to get are the body-builders. Dried eggs build muscle and repair tissue in just the same way as do chops and steaks; and are better for health-protection. So we are particularly lucky to be able to get dried eggs to make up for any shortage of other body-builders such as meat, fish, cheese, milk.

Your allowance of DRIED EGG is equal to 3 eggs a week

You can now get one 12-egg packet (price 1 3) per 4-week rationing period — three fine fresh eggs a week, at the astonishingly low price of

1½d. each. Children (holders of green ration books) get two packets each rationing period. You buy your dried eggs at the shop where you are registered for shell eggs; poultry keepers can buy anywhere.

Don't hoard your dried eggs; use them up — there are plenty more coming!

Note. *Don't make up dried eggs until you are ready to use them; they should not be allowed to stand after they've been mixed with water or other liquid. Use dry when making cakes and so on, and add a little more moisture when mixing.*

FREE — **DRIED EGG LEAFLET** containing many interesting recipes, will be sent on receipt of a postcard addressed to Dept. 627E, Food Advice Service, Ministry of Food, London, W.1.

ISSUED BY THE MINISTRY OF FOOD (S.74)

Ministry of Food pamphlet

We left our bucket with five shillings in it for a dozen

the siding in the station precincts. We then backed up on to a goods train for our journey back to Leicester, stopping at all stations to pick up or drop off the odd parcel wagon or coal wagon and pick up empties as required.

The first station we stopped at was Bottesford. After we had shunted off the coal wagons and parcel wagons we anchored the engine down. The fire in the firebox needed cleaning by this time, which meant the clinker that had built up in the firebox over the fire bars needed removing. That meant breaking it up with the straight dart – similar to a long poker with a point on the end – and lifting the lumps of the clinker from the firebox with the long fire shovel, which was kept in a rack on the tender, being careful not to drop burning clinker on to the footplate in the process. This was quite a warm job but very necessary for the efficient generation of steam in the boiler.

The term 'getting coal down' meant climbing on to the tender and shovelling coal forward to the front of the tender so that it was easily accessible when the engine was being fired. Coal tended to lie where it was put on the

BULL INN

Stan Laurel and Oliver Hardy
stayed at this 18th Century
Inn whilst appearing at
the Empire Theatre
Nottingham during
Christmas 1952

Olga Healey, sister of
Lancashire born Stan Laurel
and her husband Bill were
Licensees of the premises
during this period.

BULL
INN

The pub was run by the sister of Stanley Laurel

*I slipped across the fields to a place
where I knew that bluelegs grew*

tender and coal dust combined with the coal did not allow the coal to fall freely towards the well of the tender. Any opportunity to 'get coal down' and make firing easier was not to be missed.

While I cleaned the fire and got coal down, Harold made his way into the village of Bottesford. He took a shortcut across the graveyard of St Mary's parish church that is almost opposite the station. He went straight into the pub, the Bull Inn, which was most likely the oldest pub in Bottesford.

After I had made the engine all ready to leave I followed Harold to the pub where a pint was waiting for me on the bar. Olga Healey, the sister of Stanley Laurel, of Laurel and Hardy fame, ran the pub. Harold and I had a chinwag with Olga while we drank our beer, then made our way back across the graveyard to our waiting engine. When we got back we found that the guard was agitated, saying that if we didn't go we would be blocking the line for other trains. We thought that this was a bad habit of his!

After leaving Bottesford we carried on, stopping to pick up our eggs on the crossing just before Redmile station. We shunted the odd wagon or two in the station precincts. Whilst we were in the sidings at Redmile I took the opportunity to look round the station platform itself. Redmile is 2½ miles

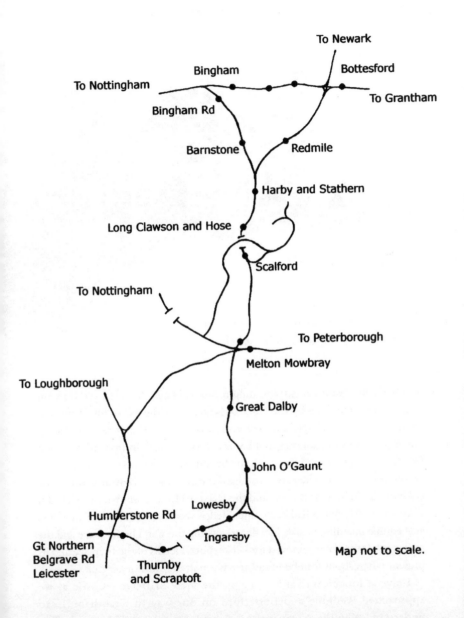

To Newark

Bottesford

Bingham

To Nottingham

To Grantham

Bingham Rd

Barnstone

Redmile

Harby and Stathern

Long Clawson and Hose

Scalford

To Nottingham

To Peterborough

Melton Mowbray

To Loughborough

Great Dalby

John O'Gaunt

Lowesby

Humberstone Rd

Ingarsby

Gt Northern
Belgrave Rd
Leicester

Thurnby
and Scraptoft

Map not to scale.

'We used to work a local passenger train, stopping at all
stations between Leicester Great Northern and Grantham'

Redmile ticket office in ruins is all that remains of the station

from Belvoir Castle. An extra waiting room had been designed and built on to the station buildings by the Duke of Rutland for the use of his family and friends, and by royalty when they visited Belvoir Castle. It was on the up line. I went into this waiting room as the door was ajar. In front of me was a fireplace and a surround that took my breath away. There was an overmantel carved out of wood. The carver had used the environs of Belvoir Castle – the castle itself, the Vale of Belvoir and the Belvoir Hunt, all shown in relief. But some of these carvings had been vandalised, it was said, by the troops stationed at Redmile guarding nearby fuel dumps during the war. The fireplace and the overmantel were later removed for safekeeping. Details of the fireplace and its present whereabouts can be found at www.bottesfordhistory.org.uk.

I always looked forward to seeing the view of Belvoir Castle as we approached Redmile and Bottesford on our way to Grantham. I can understand why the Normans chose this location to build a castle. The present castle is the fourth building to stand on the site since Norman times – a marvellous vantage point. It is a Grade I listed building. The name Belvoir means 'a beautiful view'.

There were special toilet facilities at Redmile decorated with blue and white tiles. These were possibly the blue pantiles that were made locally.

The hand basins in the toilets were pivoted at the sides and tipped up to empty, seeming quite modern to me in the 1950s. No doubt they had already been there for as many as fifty years.

After Redmile we made our way to Stathern Iron sidings where we did some more shunting. While Harold was shunting wagons with the guard, I slipped across the fields to a place where I knew that bluelegs, a variety of mushroom, grew. (The Latin name for bluelegs is *Lapista Saeva*, Field Blueit or Blueleg.) Bluelegs were only in season during November and December. They had their own unique taste. They were not grown commercially but were often seen for sale in the fruit and veg markets in Leicester through the enterprise of local farmers, who no doubt knew the market traders. During the other months, of course, we just picked mushrooms. We had the right ingredients for a tasty breakfast!

We then returned to Leicester. One of the stations we passed was John O'Gaunt. John O'Gaunt himself was the third son of Edward III and was born in 1399. He was the first Duke of Lancaster, the fifth Earl of Leicester. He was originally known as John of Ghent because he was born in Ghent and there was a locomotive named after him in 1839–40. The station opened in 1879 as the Burrow and Twyford station but was renamed John O'Gaunt in 1883. The station closed to regular traffic in 1953.

Chris has drawn a map of the line (see p.135) showing the stations from Leicester Belgrave Road to Grantham. Only two of these small stations are still in use: Bottesford and Sedgebrook. Each of the now-closed stations had a history, as John O'Gaunt had, and the line and the stations set in a rural landscape had a particular Midland charm.

16

END NOTE

While we were drinking a pint and trying to sort out winners between us from the *Racing Times*, I often reflected on what Cyril and I had just done during our shift. We were two tired footplate men sitting in the pub after experiencing all sorts of sensations, whether dealing with hazardous weather such as fog, snow and ice, or at times dangerous conditions, whilst having to push a locomotive to its limits. It hardly ever occurred to me that maybe we could hit a broken rail or something on the line as we raced along. I think the sensations I experienced, coupled with the work I had to do, negated the danger. At night the particular motion and noises of the engine – rolling, creaking, groaning – changing as the speed increased, as well as the glare and heat from the firebox, the wind, the smoke, the smell, all heightened my senses further as we flew along. On the night fast, for instance, after I had wedged myself into the best position for firing correctly (depending on the type of engine and the characteristics of the firebox) and also whilst we were moving at speed, I fired the engine. Three-cylinder engines (Pacifics) had a rolling movement – a better ride than a two-cylinder worn-out B1, which had a more jolting movement that continued in my head long after I had got down from the footplate.

A few hours before we had both travelled to work on our bikes. Cyril often visited his allotment before coming to work, bringing me apples or some other fruit as I had a young family.

The artist J.M.W. Turner illustrated the effect of power and steam and the elements in his paintings in the mid-nineteenth century. I relate to Turner and the powerful images he created. An engine in steam attracts the attention

It was a mucky, sweaty and very physical
but exciting job

of everyone on the station platform. A railway locomotive creates a cocktail of sounds: the unforgettable clickety-clack from the rails that passengers anticipate as they travel along, the quiet hiss of steam escaping from the valves and pistons as the engine sits in a bay at the station ready to take a train forward, the bark from the chimney as the engine takes load and pulls the train away from the station, the slip of the wheels before the engine gets into its stride, the familiar whistle as the train screams through stations and tunnels, and the impromptu blast of surplus steam from the safety valve that never fails to make people jump.

I found the generation of steam in the locomotive, that began with the lighting of a match together with the simple ingredients of several firelighters placed under some small cobbles, and the coal added gradually, through to the energising of a power unit capable of many horsepower, to be amazing. To try to square that with a bucking bronco of an engine charging along at 90mph is something I found exciting, exhilarating and quite unreal. The vivid images are with me still. It was a mucky, sweaty and very physical but exciting job. It could be quite dangerous if you did not have your wits about you. Somehow we always found time to laugh about our exploits and I was never bored.

Lurking around in my head during the time in which I have been writing these tales is the word 'reportage'. I have avoided reportage wherever I could. Each story starts at Leicester, spreads to other cities and towns along the line and finishes back at Leicester. By the linear nature of the railway, tales are confined to the limits of the railway network on which the trains are operating. Trains run to timetables and they stop at scheduled stations. They cannot stop where they like or indeed come off the rails. The very nature of the railway system would encourage a storyteller to use reportage, because the routes, times and whereabouts of a train, on lines, is in fact the system. The footplate man works within this system – 'I booked on at', 'we arrived on time' etc. The stories here are about the incidents that occurred within this framework.

The spectacle of a steam train approaching at speed never seems to dim. It was described to me as 'like a great fiery dragon approaching' by a lady who, as a little girl with her brother, ran down to the end of the garden every night to see the dragon go by with its 'clickety-clack, clickety-clack' and watched the train disappear into the distance.

17

I REMEMBER AS IF
IT WAS YESTERDAY

I have given the last word to my wife. This is her story:

I remember as if it was yesterday. Well, only half of that is true. I do remember it, but it does seem a long time ago. So I think I will start this tale in the way of tales of long ago, with once upon a time.

Once upon a time, in the spring of 1946, I happened to be in the right place at the right time, as they say. That is how I came to be on the Great Central Railway station platform at Leicester under the water columns, dressed in the thinnest of long cotton dresses. I was 15. I had five equally young companions, each shivering as I was in the chilly wind, who were, like me, waiting for the Railway Queen to arrive – a glamorous ambassador chosen by the railway company. The line came from Nottingham, but where it stretched further than that we did not enquire. Nottingham seemed a long way away, a very different place. The track narrowed as it disappeared round a bend on its way to Nottingham and it was in that direction that we were facing, anticipating the arrival of the train and its important passenger.

This all came about because we were members of a group who were learning to swing Indian clubs, an ancient art popular in the eastern world for health and beauty. How I came to be in the class I cannot imagine, but I think I was quite good at it. Then one day, as with all once-upon-a-time tales, the magic happened. The auburn-haired and competent leader of the group – her hair was particularly curly and memorable – had a boyfriend concerned with railway matters. As the organiser of that year's tour of the Railway Queen, he made sure that at each station she was greeted and cared

I felt like the Railway
Queen herself

for by a group of young ladies who formed her ladies-in-waiting. Our tutor offered us. We didn't decline; it was too exciting to say no. But I must say that it was difficult to explain to our friends and family that we had the correct credentials to fulfil the task ahead.

We were a motley group, but we had several things in common. We were sure that we were attractive – who would want unattractive folk around the Queen? – and as such we had to find appropriate dresses. We were also certain that we would do our prospective job properly, smile at the press photographer, be polite to the fur-coated VIP who represented Leicestershire (she also had a neat fur hat on her neatly coiffured head) and generally but certainly make our visitor feel welcome. Acquiring long dresses presented a few difficulties as none of us had worn one before and I suspect one or two of us had not even seen one before. The nearest I had got to making any sort of acquaintanceship with a long dress was my mother's wedding dress, which was long at the back but the hem was very raised at the front in the manner of fashion in the late 1920s. As a small child I had surreptitiously tried it on, loving the feel of the sequins that formed the neckline decoration. For my debut as a railway lady-in-waiting I borrowed – I had no clothing coupons for long dresses – a pale green dress that had a sweetheart neckline and small puffed, pretty sleeves with the hemline just above my ankles and I felt like the Railway Queen herself.

As the train came to a standstill there was much smoke and some fuss. The delicate, white high-heeled shoe of the Queen appeared and as she stepped gingerly and daintily down on to the platform we rose to the occasion, surrounding her in our colourful dresses, highlighting her ivory dress decorated with some glitter on that cold, grey morning and tried to make her feel at home. She was beautiful, with auburn curly hair (reminiscent of my Indian club teacher), a sweet face and a gentle smile. It had to be so. She did, in fact, look like a fairytale princess, advertising the wares of the railway line she represented with gentle aplomb. The husband of the lady VIP, who would also have been a VIP, stood with his wife. We grouped ourselves around them, the Queen stood in the centre and the cameras clicked.

Once-upon-a-time stories, however incongruous the links in them are, almost always have happy endings. This one did. I gave up the club swinging classes and found a prince instead. When he saw the photograph of the occasion, printed from the one taken by the press, he jumped with a start. 'I recognise that water tower!' he said. As part of a footplate crew he knew the route well, specially the line to Nottingham and beyond.

So I married him, and we are still living happily ever after!

If you enjoyed this book, you may also be interested in …

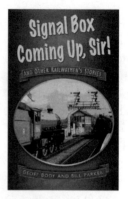

Signal Box Coming Up, Sir!
And Other Railwaymen's Stories
GEOFF BODY AND BILL PARKER

There's never a dull moment in this entertaining collection of experiences as Geoff Body and Bill Parker present often hilarious highlights from the careers of railwaymen around Britain over the last fifty years. Featuring daring robberies, royal visits, lost passengers, bomb scares, coffins, circus trains and ladies of the night, it chronicles both successes and disasters, with accounts of moving a farm and a circus, 245 miles of marooned railway, footplate adventures, animal capers and many equally fascinating subjects.

978 0 7524 6040 6

Railway Oddities
GEOFFREY BODY

Over the years railways have seen a diverse mix of traffic and many unusual events have occurred. There have been special services for Glastonbury festival goers, consignments as varied as boilers and bees, rural branches like the 'Crab & Winkle', trains to carry corpses, circus trains and unusual commercial enterprises such as excursions to watch prize fighters and cinema coaches. This compilation of titbits captures the fascination and variety of railways with over 250 accounts garnered from the press, friends and colleagues, and from the author's own experience, creating an immensely readable collection.

978 0 7524 4399 7

Visit our website and discover thousands of other History Press books.

www.thehistorypress.co.uk